The Prepper's Survival Bible

20 Books in 1 | A Complete Guide to Long Term Survival, Stockpiling, Off-Grid Living, Canning, Home Defense, Self-Sufficiency, and Other Life-Saving Strategies to Survive Anywhere

By Dale Mann

© **Copyright Dale Mann and Willow Walsh 2024 - All rights reserved.**

The content contained within this book may not be reproduced, duplicated or transmitted without direct written permission from the author or the publisher.

Under no circumstances will any blame or legal responsibility be held against the publisher, or author, for any damages, reparation, or monetary loss due to the information contained within this book. Either directly or indirectly. You are responsible for your own choices, actions, and results.

Legal Notice:

This book is copyright protected. This book is only for personal use. You cannot amend, distribute, sell, use, quote or paraphrase any part, or the content within this book, without the consent of the author or publisher.

Disclaimer Notice:

Please note the information contained within this document is for educational and entertainment purposes only. All effort has been executed to present accurate, up to date, and reliable, complete information. No warranties of any kind are declared or implied. Readers acknowledge that the author is not engaging in the rendering of legal, financial, medical or professional advice. The content within this book has been derived from various sources. Please consult a licensed professional before attempting any techniques outlined in this book.

By reading this document, the reader agrees that under no circumstances is the author responsible for any losses, direct or indirect, which are incurred as a result of the use of the information contained within this document, including, but not limited to, — errors, omissions, or inaccuracies.

Table of Contents

TABLE OF CONTENTS ....

INTRODUCTION 1

BOOK 1: THE PREPARATION: GATHERING FOOD 5

   FINDING THE RIGHT FOOD 9
      The Criteria for Choosing the Right Food 9

BOOK 2: WATER 13

   CHAPTER 1 - MAKING WATER SAFE TO CONSUME DURING EMERGENCIES 17
      Killing Parasites and Pathogens 18
      Disinfecting Water 18
      Disinfecting with Bleach 18
      Disinfecting with 1% Concentrate of Sodium Hypochlorite 19
      More Ways of Disinfecting Water 19
      Filtering Water to Make it Safe for Use 19
   CHAPTER 2 - THE ESSENTIALS OF WATER STORAGE 20

BOOK 3: THE STORAGE 21

   CHAPTER 1 - HOW TO STORE YOUR FOOD 23
      The Ideal Environment for Food Storage 23
      Humidity 23
      Oxygen 23
      Light 24
      Temperature 24
   CHAPTER 2 - POSSIBLE PLACES THAT CAN SERVE AS FOOD STORAGE 25
      Places to AVOID Using for Food Storage 25
      Freezing Food 25
      Preservation 26
      No Special Equipment 26
      No Spoilage 26
      Buy Time 26
   CHAPTER 3 - TYPES OF FOOD TO FREEZE 27
      Meat, Fish, and Poultry 27
      Fruits and Vegetables 27

Processed Fruits and Vegetables 27
Dairy Products 27
Ready to Eat Meals 28
Extras 28

CHAPTER 4 - THE TIMING OF FROZEN FOOD 29
1 to 2 Months 29
2 to 4 Months 29
4 to 6 Months 30
6+ Months 30

CHAPTER 5 - HOW TO FREEZE YOUR FOOD 31
Freezing Fruit 31
Freezing Veggies 31
Freezing Meat 31
Freezing Herbs 31

CHAPTER 6 - FREEZING TECHNIQUES 32
Contact Freezing 32
Blast Freezing 32
Brine Freezing 32
Cryogenic Freezing 32
Slow and Quick Freezing 32

CHAPTER 7 - FERMENTING FOOD 33
Types of Fermentation 33
Basic Steps to Ferment Food 34
Best Food to Ferment 35

CHAPTER 8 - -DEHYDRATING FOOD 36
Which Food can You Dehydrate? 36
The Dehydrating Process 38
The Tools Needed 38
5 Steps to Perfectly Dehydrated Food 39

BOOK 4: THE ULTIMATE PREPPER'S FOOD LIST **41**
Grains 43
Beans and Legumes 45
Fats 45
Meats and Proteins 46
Spices 47

Condiments 48
Fruits and Vegetables 48

BOOK 5: STOCKING UP ON CANNED FOOD 51

Chapter 1 - The Preparation 53
Chapter 2 - Intro to Canned Food 55
Chapter 3 - Canning Your Own Food 56
Processing 56
Sealing 56
Heating 56

Chapter 4 – The Methods of Canning 57
The Boiling Water Bath Method 57
The Pressure Canner Method 58
The Atmospheric Steam Canner Method 58
The General Canning Steps 59

Chapter 5 – Safety and Maintenance 60
Take Stock 60
Set a Budget 60
Buy Slowly and for Long-Term 60
Get Things on Sale 60
Pantry Rotation 61
How Long Does Home Canned Food Last? 62

BOOK 6: THE BEST CANNED FOOD RECIPES 63

Canned Meat 67
Canned Fruits and Vegetables 69
Canned Soups 79

BOOK 7: THE PREPARATION: THE PREPPER'S RECIPE LIST 85

The Cookbook Introduction 88
Outdoor Grill 88
Swedish Fire Log Candle 88
Rocket Stove 88
Hobo Stove 88
Dutch Oven 88
Wood Burning Stove 88

Chapter 1 – The Prepper's Breakfast 90

Cornmeal Mush *90*

Corn Dodgers *90*

Cured Bacon *91*

Hasty Bread *92*

Chapter 2 – The Prepper's Lunch 93

2-Ingredient Beef Stew *93*

Prepper's Pizza *93*

Chicken and Dumplings *94*

Lemony Chicken Pasta *94*

Jerky Gravy *95*

Chapter 3 – The Prepper's Dinner 97

5-Ingredient Mac & Cheese *97*

Pasta and Red Sauce *97*

Cream of Mushroom Soup *98*

Corned Beef *98*

Potato Cakes *99*

Chapter 4 – The Prepper's Snacks 100

Hardtack *100*

Traditional Pemmican *100*

Jerky *101*

Bannock *102*

Dried Fruit *103*

Ration Bars *104*

Chapter 5 – The Prepper's Dessert 105

Chocolate Syrup *105*

Raspberry Crumble Bars *106*

Rice Pudding *107*

BOOK 8: THE DEFENSE: PROTECTING YOUR HOME 109

The Defense Introduction 113

During Vacation *114*

An Open Garage Door *114*

Windows *115*

Doors Around Your Home *115*

The Rear Door *115*

Chapter 1 – The Outdoor Defense 117

Not Leaving Your Keys Outside 117

Never Put Your Name and Address on Your Keys 117

Ensuring Your Outdoor Areas are Well Lit 117

Keeping Your Outdoor Spaces Neat 118

Securing Your Mail 118

Being Cautious of People Who Come up to Your Door 118

Enhancing Your Landscape for Security 118

Setting Alarms on Your Driveway 119

Installing Fences 120

Adding Locks to Your Gates 120

CHAPTER 2 – THE INDOOR DEFENSE 121

Securing Your Doors 121

Securing Sliding Glass Doors 121

Securing Your Garage 122

Securing Your Windows 122

Installing Security Alarms and Cameras 123

Getting a Guard Dog 123

CHAPTER 3 – THE DETERRENTS 124

Home Security System 124

Warning Signs 124

Evidence of a Guard Dog 125

Anti-Climb Spikes 125

Bulletproof or Tempered Glass 125

A Licensed Gun 126

Home Traps 126

BOOK 9: THE DEFENSE: HEALING YOURSELF 129

THE MEDICINAL INTRODUCTION 133

Natural Medicine and its History 133

CHAPTER 1 - BENEFITS OF NATURAL MEDICINE 135

CHAPTER 2 - NATURAL MEDICINE FOR PREPPERS 136

CHAPTER 3 - FAQS ABOUT PREPARING FOR EMERGENCIES WITH NATURAL MEDICINE 138

BOOK 10 – ALL ABOUT NATURAL MEDICINE 141

Being Safe While Using Herbal Medicine 143

CHAPTER 1 - THE TOOLS OF NATURAL MEDICINE 144

CHAPTER 2 - HERBAL REMEDIES USING COMMON SPICES 146

Common Medicinal Herbs 147

CHAPTER 3 - USEFUL INGREDIENTS FOR MAKING HOMEMADE HERBAL REMEDIES 148

BOOK 11 – GROWING YOUR OWN HERB GARDEN 149

Identifying the Herbs that Grow Well in Your Area's Climate 151

Locate Your Garden Zone 151

Map Out Your Landscape 152

Determine the Amount of Each Herb You Need 152

BOOK 12 – THE NATURAL MEDICINE REMEDIES 153

CHAPTER 1 - A NATURAL MEDICINE LIST 156

CHAPTER 2 - THE AILMENTS AND THEIR MEDICINES 187

CHAPTER 3 - THE HERBAL MEDICINE DOSAGE 191

BOOK 13 – THE ULTIMATE PREPPER'S MEDICINE LIST 193

CHAPTER 1 - OVER-THE-COUNTER (OTC) MEDICATION 196

CHAPTER 2 - THE MEDICAL KIT 199

BOOK 14: THE LIFESTYLE: LIVING OFF THE GRID 203

THE OFF-GRID LIVING INTRODUCTION 207

CHAPTER 1 – TACKLING THE MYTHS ABOUT OFF-GRID LIVING 208

CHAPTER 2 - THE PROS AND CONS OF LIVING OFF THE GRID 211

The Pros 211

The Cons 211

CHAPTER 3 – PREPARING FOR OFF-GRID LIVING 213

Things to Consider 213

Steps to Take for Off-Grid Living 214

CHAPTER 4 – THE DETAILS OF OFF-GRID LIVING 217

Types of Houses 217

Electricity 218

Finding Food 218

Finding Water 219

Cooking 220

BOOK 15 – WASTE & HYGIENE 221

The Steps to Managing Waste 223

Start Sorting 223

Composting Food Waste 223

Burning Waste 224

Reduce Waste 225

Bury Waste 225

Burying Human Waste 225

Staying Clean off the Grid 226

BOOK 16: THE LIFESTYLE: SURVIVING AS LONG AS POSSIBLE 227

CHAPTER 1 – THE BEGINNING OF YOUR PREPARATION 231

The SHTF Scenarios 231

Preparing for the Worst 232

Extra Preparedness Steps 234

CHAPTER 2 – THE SCENARIOS 237

The General Preparation Steps 237

Scenario #1: Natural Disasters 238

Scenario #2: War 239

Scenario #3: Global Warming 240

Scenario #4: Economic Collapse 241

Scenario #5: Pandemic 242

BOOK 17 – BUGGING IN AND BUGGING OUT 243

CHAPTER 1 - BUGGING IN 246

CHAPTER 2 - BUGGING OUT 248

BOOK 18: THE LIFESTYLE: LIFE-SAVING STRATEGIES 251

THE IMPORTANCE OF LIFE-SAVING SKILLS 256

Earns You Mileage in Life 256

Easy to Learn 256

Helps get You Away from Disasters 256

Prevents Suffering and Helps You Heal Faster 256

Places You in a Position to Possibly Save a Life 256

Helps Boost Self-Worth 257

Invaluable Knowledge 257

Offers the Ability to Prevent Health Emergencies 257

BOOK 19 – SPECIFIC SKILLS TO LEARN FOR DISASTERS 259

CHAPTER 1 - FINDING SHELTER 261

Tree and Bushes 261

 Hollowed Logs 261
 Tarp Shelters 262
 Snow Trenches 262
 Lean-to 263
 Chapter 2 - Staying Warm 264
  Creating a Fire 264
  Tea Candles 265
  Survival Blankets 265
  Newspapers or Plastic Sheets 265
  Hand Warmers 265
  Hot Stones 265
  Passive Exercise 266
 Chapter 3 - Cooling Off 267
  Avoiding the Sun 267
  Stay Hydrated 267
  Frozen Treats 268
  Cooling Sheets and Pillows 268
  Fans 268
  Spray Bottles 268

BOOK 20 – THE LIFE-SAVING SKILLS YOU NEED 271

 Chapter 1 - Life-Saving First-Aid Skills 274
 Chapter 2 - Life-Saving Skills in the Wilderness 276
 Chapter 3 - Marking Your Waypoints 278
 Chapter 4 - Life-Saving Skills for Weapons and Protection 281
 Chapter 5 - Life-Saving Skills for Food 282
 Chapter 6 - Extra Life-Saving Skills 283

CONCLUSION 285

 Preppers Can Make It Through The Unfathomable 286
  Anyone Can Be A Prepper 286
  What Are Preppers Preparing to Survive? 287

REFERENCES 290

FREE GIFT TO OUR READER

PREPPER'S JOURNAL PDF DOWNLOAD

Introduction

"There's no harm in hoping for the best as long as you're prepared for the worst."
– Stephen King

Did you know that it is estimated that there are between 5 and 15 million preppers in the USA alone? That figure is growing year by year, showing a significant spike since 2020. That number only grows on the international scale.

These people believe in taking responsibility for their safety, as well as the well-being of their loved ones and being self-sufficient, no matter the event. That is their commonality, but they come from different walks of life, different cultures, different affiliations, and different backgrounds. The man sitting next to you on the train with a preppy suit and tie can be a prepper, and so could the lady who sells your favorite apples down at the farmers' market. The businesswoman living in a high-rise condo in New York City could be a prepper, so, too, could be the man who has chosen to live in a small cabin in the middle of the woods with no immediate neighbors. Every day, people that you pass on the street and bump figurative elbows with online could be preppers. There is no physical appearance or way of life that comes with being one, only a particular mindset for preparation before a disaster happens.

Before the Covid-19 pandemic hit, preppers and survivalists were often mocked by their family and peers. This mindset of being ever-ready was seen as alien, and many people did not know how to relate to that. They saw such preparation as extreme. Gearing up for an apocalyptic event was the stuff reserved for a movie script—so cliché and laughable.

But then the Covid-19 pandemic hit the globe in March 2020, and those who snickered at such extremes were wishing that they were as prepared as people whom they saw on TV shows like *Doomsday Preppers*. Survivalists and preppers were definitely advanced when it came to dealing with this unprecedented time.

The pandemic forced us into our homes and showed that only the fittest and most prepared survived, as grocery shelves were wiped out instantly with panic-buying. People lost jobs and their means of income, and they had no contingency plans to survive. People were unsure of how to handle medical emergencies with first responders caught up in handling the fallout of the sheer numbers swarming the hospitals. Most of us had been living comfortable lives before the pandemic but, seemingly overnight, there was the threat of all our basic necessities being taken away.

Covid-19 was certainly an "eye-opener", and the sight was ghastly as to how woefully unprepared most people were as everything we knew as "normal" suddenly fell apart. The pandemic also highlighted that an apocalyptic event can happen at any time. It was Covid-19 then (and still is many years after), but with the threat of wars, climate change, classism, inequality, and so many other events that can spell disaster, the worst can happen at any time, and we need to be prepared *before* it happens again.

In such states of emergencies, we cannot rely on our governments to help us survive. We cannot rely on emergency systems and frontlines to respond to us personally when such events most likely mean that they will be overwhelmed. We need to be able to fend for *ourselves*.

This book was written to help you be prepared to face any kind of "storm".

It is frightening, isn't it? Living through a historic event like the Covid-19 pandemic? Every single person on this planet has been negatively impacted in one way or the other. We all know someone who has died from the virus. We know someone who has been sick from the symptoms, if we haven't been sick ourselves. We know people who have lost their livelihoods and even been kicked out of their homes. We know people who have been victimized because of their exposure to different aspects of this virus. We know people who have gone without meals and do not know where their next one will come from.

Even years later, life has not settled back into "normal," and it does not look like it ever will. The government has not been able to contain this pandemic and its effects on everyday citizens. We have needed to work around inconveniences and tragedies because life continues and never stops. So yes, it is all scary, and you have every right to feel fear and worry. We have seen the need to be prepared for events like this because it is not just isolated to history books anymore. We are living through them, and we need to be prepared to survive, and not just survive by our bootstraps, either.

This preparation is not just for us but also for our kids and future generations. We need to ensure that our children have a life worth looking forward to living if things get worse with this pandemic or some other catastrophic event.

But being a prepper is not as easy as they make it seem in the media, as many of us have realized as the pandemic has forced us to transition into the lifestyle. It takes work and a willingness to learn, adapt, and embrace things outside of what we were taught is normal. But you no longer have to fumble in the dark. This book was written to help you prepare yourself, your family, and your home for disasters. You no longer have to feel the grip of panic in your chest in uncertain situations because, by the time you get to the last page of this book, you will have the confidence that you will be prepared to handle any off-the-wall situation, even if it is as far-fetched as a zombie outbreak.

This book is comprehensive so that you really do learn how to survive in any situation. In fact, 8 different books have been condensed into this one space to teach you (to name a few) how to:

- Gather safe-to-consume food and water.
- Stock up so that you are not reliant on food from grocery shelves at any given moment.
- Physically defend yourself and your loved ones against natural disasters and intruders.
- Treat yourself medicinally with natural remedies.
- Live comfortably and sustainably off the grid.

- And more!

I have even included recipes that you can easily prepare so that your taste buds do not have to suffer.

The thing many people do not understand is that preppers are not living in a fear-filled state of mind about what could happen. Rather, they live with a mindset of ease because they are not worried about their ability to survive in case the worst happens. They erased that fear by gaining confidence in knowing that they have the tools, the skills, and the mindset necessary to get through any situation. That is the mental place this book aims to bring you to.

You can build a sustainable life where your pantry is stocked. Where you don't have to worry about where you will get food and safe drinking water at any given time. Where you are confident that you can ward off danger no matter what environment you find yourself in. Where you can get out of the concrete jungle and the rat race, if that is your choice, and still live happily in the wild. You can do all of this and more without giving up the comforts of life as you know it now. In fact, I, as a prepper myself, can vouch when I say that you will live happier and more fulfilled in your everyday life as you eliminate the fear of being unable to handle uncertainty. That is the power of being a prepper—you live without fear and worry because you know you got this no matter what!

Turn the page and let's get started transitioning you into the lifestyle where fear and worry are no longer constant companions.

Book 1:
The Preparation: Gathering Food

In 2013, Gene Penaflor was lost in the wilderness of a nature preserve in northern California for almost 3 weeks; 19 days, to be precise. Let's start from the beginning to illustrate how this happened and how this man miraculously survived.

72 years old at the time, Gene was out hunting for deer with his friend, from whom he got separated as the two people flanked a deer from different directions. The two were supposed to meet up at a planned spot a few hours later and, while Gene's friend arrived according to plan, Gene did not make it. His friend did the responsible thing and reported Gene missing a day later. A search party was organized and law officials and rescue dogs inspected every nook and cranny along the mountain range by foot and by air for 4 days. There was no sign of Gene, and then a storm blew in, causing the search to become suspended. The snowstorm was so bad that temperatures dropped to 25 degrees Fahrenheit many nights.

The question on everyone's mind: where was Gene?

While Gene had been pursuing the deer, he had walked out into the wilderness farther than he had planned. If that wasn't bad enough, he slipped down a slope and hit his head on the way down. The fall had knocked him out cold, so much so that he had no idea for how long he had been unconscious.

Understanding that his situation was dangerous indeed, Gene went into survival mode and prioritized conserving his energy in his injured state. For sustenance, he foraged for algae in a nearby stream and hunted small game with his hunting rifle. On the list of game that he ate were squirrels, lizards, and frogs. To keep hydrated, he drank water from a creek. He kept himself protected from the worst of the elements by taking shelter under a fallen tree and keeping warm with a fire that he made. He also packed grass and dry leaves around his body to keep his body temperature up.

Gene could have easily panicked and gone off on a tangent. Instead, he kept his cool and used reason to keep himself alive. He knew that his family would send help for him. All he had to do was stay alive until that help came. After the storm had passed, authorities once again resumed the search, but it was not law officials who found Gene. Instead, it was a group of hunters who stumbled upon him. They heard the man crying for help down in a valley and managed to call for emergency assistance, despite a spotty cell phone connection.

The hunting party was crafty indeed as they made a makeshift stretcher to pull Gene out of the area that he had fallen into. Official help caught up to the hunting group and their rescue a few hours later, after which Gene was transported to a nearby medical center via helicopter. Luckily, Gene was not the worse for wear and, after checking him off, doctors gave him the all-clear to go home to his relieved family.

Gene's story is a true inspiration because, despite having the odds stacked against him, he made it out alive because of a mindset to survive.

Let's look at all the things he did right to ensure that he survived. First and foremost, he ensured that he had food and water.

The human body can live up to 3 weeks without food, provided that you have water to drink. On the other hand, without both food and water, it is unlikely that a person will live past 4 days. Even with water, the body undergoes severe negative outcomes without food, such as a dramatic loss in body mass. This is because the body starts to break down its own tissue for energy. This leads to a disruption in all vital processes, like metabolism, digestion, respiration, responsiveness, and movement. Therefore, not only do you suffer from severe weight loss, but going without food for longer than a few days can also lead to organ failure.

Gene ensured that this did not happen to him to the best of his abilities under these dire circumstances by hunting game that provided him with a source of protein and fat, as well as algae, which was a source of vitamins and minerals. Without these, along with water, Gene would have wasted away, even if he had the means of surviving the snowstorm.

This book is geared toward helping you find the right food, a water source, and the right way to store food for disasters. Let's dive right into part one, which is all about sourcing food.

Finding the Right Food

Access to food is a must. After all, without food, there would be no human life. In fact, human beings will not survive more than a few days without food. Access to food is a must-have to remain in good health, right up there with access to clean water, clean air, shelter, and clothing.

Human nature is such that one of our first instincts is to store food during a disaster. Therefore, it is no surprise, with this new mindset for preparedness before the worst happens, that food is one of the first considerations. But you cannot just pick food at random and tick this must-do off your prepper's list. Doing so runs the risk of you having food that has spoiled long before you need it most.

There are two basic strategies that you can employ to ensure that you have food saved up for times of emergency. The first is to store extra non-perishable food with a long shelf life for everyday use. Such food can be accessed by simply going on a grocery run to your local supermarket.

Even though the average American household has less than 3 days' worth of food and water stored up, it is ideal that you have at least enough food and water to last you for 2 weeks. This is because, in extreme situations and disasters such as earthquakes and hurricanes, supermarket food supplies are often disrupted and store shelves are quickly emptied.

Food supplies can also become tainted because of circumstances such as flooding, which contaminates items on grocery shelves. You need to be able to survive on a daily basis if those became circumstances that you suffer through.

The second strategy for having a food supply saved up is to buy "special" food for survival that you do not crack open unless circumstances have reached a life or death status. These types of food typically last longer than the food that you buy at your local supermarket. An example of this "special" food includes MREs (Meal, Ready to Eat). These are individual, self-contained rationed food items that come in lightweight packaging. They are sold for military use, but you can access your own similar buys in the form of emergency food kits. You can purchase these at retail stores such as Costco and Walmart, as well as on online stores such as Amazon.com.

While some preppers choose either/or of these options, my advice is to use both so that you are prepared no matter what emergency life throws at you.

The Criteria for Choosing the Right Food

We understand the importance of having food stored for emergencies. However, simply throwing items together will not work. It would truly be a tragedy if you were to take that strategy only to find that most of your food has spoiled within a few days and left you back at square one—hungry and in danger of starvation.

Luckily, there are criteria that allow you to choose the right food items that will taste good and give you the nutrition you need.

Shelf Life

Quantity is not the biggest consideration when it comes to picking the right foods for keeping on hand in case of emergencies. How long these foods last is the first thing you need to think about. We never know when a disaster will strike, and it would be highly inconvenient to constantly restock foods because they have expired.

Therefore, the best course of action is to choose foods that have a long shelf life. Shelf life refers to the length of time that an item remains safely usable and fit for human consumption.

MREs can last for several years but their temperature sensitivity can severely shorten this time.

Food kits that have been created especially for survival tend to have shelf lives ranging between 20 and 30 years. Be sure to check the shelf life of the items that you are buying. They need to have shelf lives of at least a few years.

How you store food also affects its shelf life. Therefore, you do not have to rely strictly on store-bought food to make sure that you have the right food on hand. Methods like freeze-drying, canning, and vacuum-sealing can significantly increase the shelf life of food that you enjoy regularly.

Did you know that freeze-dried food can last up to 25 years? Better yet, you can freeze dry a variety of items, from coffee, fruits, vegetables, and juices to meats, fish, dairy, and seafood. Unopened canned foods tend to last for at least 1 to 2 years. Frozen, vacuum-sealed food last between 2 and 3 years on average.

Storage Capabilities

How easy food is to store needs to be on the top of your list of criteria when it comes to choosing food. Electric power can be cut off for a significant amount of time, depending on the type of emergency that you are faced with. It is not a good idea to rely entirely on cold and frozen food, even though they can have a long shelf life when they are kept cold or frozen. Storing cold and frozen goods is not totally off the table if you take secondary precautions like having a backup energy supply, such as a generator, instead of electricity gained from power lines.

However, you do not have to worry about the electricity supply with canned and boxed food because they are secured in durable packaging.

Ease of Preparation

In addition to not having a steady electricity supply, the water supply may also be interrupted during disasters. In such cases, your stored food will be no good to you if it requires water and electricity to prepare for consumption. As a result, it is best to store food that requires as little preparation as possible. Many food kits contain items that only require you to add water to freeze-dried meals. The instructions will specify whether this water needs to be at room temperature or boiled.

You do not have to totally go without a hot-cooked meal during trying times, though. Remember, it is all about preparation. Also, have a backup method of cooking. A camping stove and a gas tank make an excellent choice, and you can cook if the power is out. All you have to do is ensure you have an emergency water supply stored up. We will discuss this later.

In a pinch, you can also use alternative heat supplies, like candles, a barbecue, a wood stove, or a fireplace to heat water and cook a meal quickly. But the point of making sure food is prepared beforehand is to ensure that you do not have to rely on makeshift methods to remain nourished and healthy.

Nutritional Value

Living through a disaster is scary and takes an emotional toll. Therefore, having comfort food stored is not something that I would strictly advise against. Getting that kick of sugar from a chocolate bar or tasting the salty delight from a bag of potato chips might just be the thing that helps you keep a cool head under hard circumstances.

However, balance is key and, in this case, the scale needs to be tipped toward having healthy options. You can't rely on living off junk food no matter the situation. You still need to maintain getting nutrition from all the food groups, namely:

- Proteins
- Carbohydrates
- Dairy
- Vegetables
- Fruits
- Healthy fats and sugars

Be sure that your stored food contains items from each of these groups, not only to maintain your physical function but also your mental function, as a sound mind relies on a healthy body.

Calorie Density

Calories are units of energy that allow us to partake in any physical activity. You need calories to run. You need calories to simply move your arm by an inch. You need calories to take every breath.

We get calories from the food that we eat and the liquids that we drink. The most common way that the body gets calories is by breaking down carbohydrates in the process of metabolism. However, we can also get the calories from the fats and proteins that we consume.

Even though we need calories for every physical activity that we perform, consuming more calories than your body needs (and yes, there is a healthy limit) means that you will gain weight and run into health issues. On the other hand, consuming fewer calories than you need means that you will most likely weigh less than recommended for your body type and your health needs.

Your body size, age, gender, and physical activity level are all factors that determine the number of calories that you need to consume on a daily basis. Even under emergency situations, the number of calories that you consume needs to be considered, as you do not want unhealthy weight gain, nor do you want to be in a deficit position energy-wise.

Stay away from foods that provide empty calories. Empty calories are food and drinks that contain little to no nutritional value. Such food and drinks include desserts like cakes, candies, and soft drinks. Instead, focus on stocking up on calorie-dense food. These pack nutrient value and, thus, calories into fewer spaces. This means that you can build up your pantry even more. Examples of calorie-dense food include proteins, like eggs and carbohydrates like brown rice.

Dietary Restrictions

Most people cannot afford to pick and choose the food that they eat in an emergency situation, but some people have no choice. Having dietary issues, like being lactose or gluten intolerant means that certain foods are off the menu. Other factors, like food being discouraged by one's faith, and food simply being so hated that you cannot keep it down, limits what makes it into your emergency stash. Be familiar with yours and your family's intolerances and the food that you would like to avoid while developing your emergency pantry.

A comprehensive list of foods that are best to store (and fit into the above-stated categories) will be provided at the end of this book.

Book 2:
Water

Even before food, there is one item that you must confirm is in your supply during an emergency, and that is clean drinking water and a means to obtain more, such as a quality water filter.

Water-related emergencies can completely take away your (and an entire communities') water supply, and they are most likely to happen without notice.

Consuming contaminated water can lead to sickness and even death.

Contamination can be caused by natural disasters, like floods and hurricanes. But that is not all. This contamination can also be a result of man's actions, like waterborne disease outbreaks, chemical spills, and pollution.

Running water will not be available from taps in these cases, and others. Therefore, securing your own water supply is very important.

How much do you need to store to be on the safe side? At least a 2-week supply must be kept with at least 1 gallon (minimum) of water available for every person to use per day for sanitation and drinking, is my advice. At the bare minimum, ensure that everyone in your household has this supply for at least 3 days. In hotter climates, and if your household has pregnant or sick people, you need to bump up that amount per person.

Unopened bottled water is your best bet as a source of clean water. It is safe and can be stored for relatively long periods. Most bottled water has an expiration date of 2 years after its initial bottling. Ensure you note this expiration date when buying bottled water.

You do not have to rely on bottled water as your only source of water. You can also make most water safe for consumption.

Chapter 1 - Making Water Safe to Consume During Emergencies

Having bottled water is the best option for sourcing a safe water supply during an emergency. However, there are times when it is not possible to have that supply on hand. In such situations, you can look for a clean, safe supply inside and outside your home.

Possible sources of clean water in your home include:

- Melting ice cubes that have not been contaminated in any way, such as with chemicals.
- Residual water in your water heater.
- Liquid from canned vegetables and fruits.
- Water from your toilet tank. This water must be clear and not chemically treated.
- Water from swimming pools and spas. These can only be used for personal hygiene and cleaning. These sources must not be used for drinking unless you have a quality filter rated to remove chlorine and other types of common chemicals added to them.

Never use water from radiators.

When it is not possible to get water inside your home, you have to look outside. Possible sources of water outside your home include:

- Rainwater
- Natural springs
- Ponds
- Lakes
- Wells
- River
- Streams

These sources should only be used if they have not been contaminated by chemicals, fuel, radioactive materials, or other pollutants, AND MUST BE BOILED OR FILTERED BEFORE CONSUMING. Tap water may also need to be treated, as it may not be safe to drink after emergencies, like floods and a water main break.

Treatment to make water safe for consumption includes these processes:

- Boiling
- Disinfecting
- Filtering
- Storage

Let's look at the specifics of each step.

Killing Parasites and Pathogens

Making water sourced inside or outside of your home safe to drink means that you must ensure any disease-causing entities, such as viruses, bacteria and parasites are killed. The process for doing so is quite simple. All you have to do is boil the water.

Before boiling the water, however, if it is cloudy, you must filter it using a paper towel, a clean towel, or a coffee filter. Alternately, you can allow the water to stand so that the solid matter settles to the bottom. Extract the clear water to proceed to the boiling process.

Step one includes transferring the clear water to a clean pot and bringing it to a boil. Ensure that the water boils for 1 minute. You must see rolling bubbles during that time. If you are at an elevation above 6500 feet, increase this time to 3 minutes. Allow the water to cool completely then store it. The specific nature of safe water storage will be discussed shortly.

Disinfecting Water

Boiling water may not always be possible during an emergency, and so you need another way to make water safe for use and for drinking. Disinfection allows you to do so.

Before we proceed to how you can disinfect your water please note that if water is contaminated by harmful chemicals or radioactive materials, disinfectants will not make it safe for consumption. I reiterate this: **never use water that has been infected with toxic chemicals or radioactive material.**

You can disinfect water using either bleach or a 1% concentration of sodium hypochlorite. Let's look at how you can proceed with the disinfection process with each of these solutions.

Disinfecting with Bleach

Just like with boiling, ensure that, if the water is cloudy, it is allowed to settle or you remove any solid matter using a paper towel, clean cloth, or a coffee filter. Extract the clear water then proceed.

Typically, bleach brands have instructions for disinfecting drinking water on their labels. Simply follow these directions. If directions are not immediately clear on the label, ensure that the active ingredient is 5% - 9% sodium hypochlorite concentrate. Add an appropriate amount of bleach to the water as stated below:

- 1 quart or 1 liter of water - 2 drops if using a dropper or 0.1 ml. The amount used would be too small to be measured with a teaspoon.
- 1 gallon of water - 8 drops if using a dropper, ⅛ teaspoon, or 0.5 ml.
- 5 gallons of water - 40 drops if using a dropper, ½ teaspoon, or 2.5 ml.

Stir the water and bleach to mix well and allow to stand for 30 minutes before you drink. Store in a safe, clean container.

Disinfecting with 1% Concentrate of Sodium Hypochlorite

If you live in the USA, it is more common to find bleach compared to a 1% concentration of sodium hypochlorite, but this is certainly applicable to persons who live outside the US.

If the water being disinfected is cold or cloudy to begin with, add double the amount of the concentrate listed below:

- 1 quart or 1 liter of water - 10 drops if using a dropper, ⅛ teaspoon, or 0.5 ml.
- 1 gallon of water - 40 drops if using a dropper, ½ teaspoon, or 02.5 ml.
- 5 gallons of water - 200 drops if using a dropper, 2 ½ teaspoons, or 12.5 ml.

More Ways of Disinfecting Water

If you have chemical tablets on hand, you can also use this to disinfect water. While not a typical item on hand in the US, they are common among hikers and campers.

Other possible methods of disinfecting water include using ultraviolet light (UV light) and solar disinfection.

Using UV light includes using portable units, but these do not work well in murky water because the small particles will block out the disinfecting power of the light. Of course, you can increase the disinfecting power by allowing cloudy water to settle first or using a clean towel, a coffee filter, or a paper towel to remove the solid particles.

Solar disinfection involves using the power of the sun to kill parasites and pathogens. Fill clear plastic bottles with clear water and allow them to sit in the sun for at least 6 hours on sunny days or 2 days on cloudy days. Place the plastic bottles on a dark surface.

These last methods, of course, are only to be used in extreme emergency situations.

Filtering Water to Make it Safe for Use

As mentioned earlier, in a pinch, you can remove solid particulates from water with paper towels, a clean cloth, or a coffee filter. Step up your filter game by using a portable water filter. In addition to removing solid particles, it allows you to remove disease-causing parasites, as well, mainly giardia and cryptosporidium. Ensure that you use a filter pore size of one micron or smaller for maximum effectiveness. Note that water filters do not remove viruses or bacteria, so after the water has been filtered, either disinfect or boil as stated above.

Chapter 2 - The Essentials of Water Storage

After your water has been boiled or disinfected, you need to store it in a safe container. But what constitutes a safe water storage container? This does have to get complicated. The best option for safe water storage is FDA-approved, food-grade water storage containers. They do not hold toxic substances that can transfer into your water. You can purchase these at most camping supplies stores.

If you do not have food-grade water storage containers, the next best option must have the following qualities:

- Made out of an unbreakable and durable material. Never use glass containers.
- Have a top that can be tightly closed.
- Have a narrow opening or neck so that water can be poured out easily.

Under no circumstances should you use containers that have been previously used to hold toxic solids or liquids. For example, a container that previously contained bleach or pesticides should not be used to store water that you intend to drink or use to prepare food.

Water storage containers should be cleaned before you pour water into them. To do this, follow the next few steps:

- Wash and rinse the storage container with water.
- Create a sanitizing solution by mixing 1 teaspoon of unscented household chlorine bleach with 5% - 9% sodium hydrochloride with 1 quart of water.
- Pour the sanitizing solution into the container, cover, and shake well so that the solution touches all the inside surfaces.
- Allow the container to sit for 30 seconds then rinse out the sanitizing solution.
- Either rinse out the empty container with safe, clean, *treated* water or allow it to air dry before using.
- Pour your clean, treated water into the sanitized container and cover tightly.

Stored water should be replaced every 6 months. They should not be stored in direct sunlight nor should they be stored in the same area that is used to house toxic chemicals or substances, like pesticides or fuel. Ensure that they are kept in an area with a cool temperature between 50 and 70 degrees Fahrenheit.

Labeling is also important so that you keep track of what the water is used for. For example, water that you intend to use for consumption should be labeled "drinking water," while water to be used for hygiene should be labeled accordingly. Include the storage date on this label for easy replacement after 6 months.

How you access the water in these storage containers is also important. Never scoop out the water from the container using your hands, as you will undo the entire process of making it safe for use. Your hands can easily transfer contaminants into the water. Remove the water out of the container using a clean scoop, cup, or another similar device. Use a clean scoop with every removal.

Book 3:
The Storage

Chapter 1 - How to Store Your Food

What food items you store in preparation for a disaster is important. Where and how you store them is equally important because, even though these items have a long shelf life and meet all the other criteria that we started talking about earlier, they will spoil if they are not stored properly.

The Ideal Environment for Food Storage

There are four conditions that are ideal for your food to hold up and live out its shelf life. These factors are the humidity, oxygen, light, and temperature. Let's explore each of these factors and how you can develop the right condition for the place that you choose to store your food.

Humidity

The presence of moisture (humidity) can cause the cells inside of your food to become too filled with water, and thus, explode. This leads to spoilage. As a result, it is pertinent that you keep the area where you store the food dry. Do not keep your food near a water heater, drier, where there may be leaks, or any other place where moisture is present.

There are additional methods that you can use to keep your food dry, and they include:

- Using a low-temperature oven or a dehydrator to remove moisture from food before placing it in storage.
- Not washing any of the food before you store it in this area, as this promotes the formation of mold to rise in the humidity level.
- Keeping your storage area airy and well-ventilated.

Oxygen

There are several ways in which the presence of oxygen can cause food to spoil, and they include:

- Encouraging the growth of microorganisms that lead to yeast and mold growth.
- Interacting with the fats in food, which leads to the emission of foul odors and the creation of an off flavor.
- Speeding up chemical reactions in food. This causes browning and the development of foul odors.

Luckily, there are a variety of ways that you can deprive your food of oxygen. Such methods include smoking, canning, and vacuum sealing packaged food.

Light

Both the presence of natural sunlight and artificial light can cause food to spoil in a process called photodegradation. Photodegradation causes the substances in food, like vitamins, to change their basic chemical structure. The best way to combat this is to keep your food stored in a dark area with no windows. Step this practice up by not storing food in glass or plastic containers.

Temperature

Keeping food at too high or too low of a temperature can both cause spoilage. Ideally, it is best to keep food stored at a temperature no less than 65 degrees F. The season plays a role in how you need to adjust your thermostat. Cooler and cold months, like fall, spring, and winter often mean that you do not have to rely on your home's internal cooling as much. That may not be the case in summer. Understandably, it can be quite costly to store food at a temperature of 65 degrees F then, but keep the temperature as cool as you can afford to and can personally tolerate. Ensure that this temperature does not fluctuate.

Chapter 2 - Possible Places that can Serve as Food Storage

With all of these factors considered, some spaces fit into the criteria list quite nicely. Such spaces include:

- Basement - Ensure this space is free of dryer vents and furnace, and that you're all set to make use of it for food storage.
- Root Cellar - Ensure that this space is temperature-controlled and has shelving units installed.
- Spare Bedroom - As much as possible, ensure this space does not have windows. If it does, use heavy curtains to keep the sunlight out. Modify the space by adding shelving and other storage units to store the food.
- Closet - You can easily modify such a space by adding shelves and a lock on the door to keep your food well-organized and safe.
- Pantry - This is the ideal space in the kitchen because it is located away from sources of moisture, like the sink and refrigerator. Just like the closet space, add a lock and shelving, and you're all set.

Places to AVOID Using for Food Storage

In the same breath, there are spaces that simply do not make good storage based on the ideal conditions listed above. Some of these spaces are:

- Garage - Temperature and light conditions typically fluctuate in garages.
- Outside Shed - Inconsistent temperatures will shorten your food's shelf life in such an environment.
- Laundry Room - The presence of moisture is a food killer here.
- Bathroom - This space also contains too much moisture.
- Attic - This space is normally not well-ventilated enough and fluctuates in temperature levels. Conditions unsuitable for prolonging the shelf life of your food.

Freezing Food

Excluding circumstances where electricity may be cut off, freezing food is one of the best methods of keeping some of the items you love, want, and need readily available. Even that situation can be mitigated by having a generator handy so that you are not dependent on the electric company to keep your freezer cold.

Some of the advantages of freezing include:

Preservation

Freezing prevents the growth of microorganisms, and so your food remains fresh for longer. It also preserves the nutritional content of food.

No Special Equipment

Freezers are quite a common appliance and easy to purchase.

No Spoilage

It extends the shelf life of food. For example, fresh fruit will spoil within days, but freezing it can make it last for months and even years. This also reduces food wastage, as you do not have to throw out food unnecessarily and can make use of leftovers.

Buy Time

You can purchase food that is already frozen and simply pack it into your freezer. This is economical and also saves you time when preserving large amounts of food.

There are a few disadvantages to preserving food by freezing and this list includes:
- The process can change the texture of food.
- If food has been thawed, it cannot be refrozen, as this is not a healthy practice.
- The quality of some food will be diminished when they are frozen.

Chapter 3 - Types of Food to Freeze

Weighing the pros against the cons, it is quite obvious that freezing is a practice that a prepper can rely on to preserve food.

So, what types of foods are best to freeze? While factoring (and reducing the possibility of) the disadvantages, like change in texture and diminished quality of food, some of the food that you will have the most luck freezing includes:

Meat, Fish, and Poultry

Whether you gain these items by your own hand, like through hunting, or buy them at the local grocer, freezing them can make them last for years after you place them in the freezer ... and they will be almost as fresh as the day you placed them in the appliance, only if properly sealed (i.e.; vacuum sealed). (Freezer burn occurs when oxygen contacts frozen meats, such as from leaving in original store packaging.)

Freezing these also buys you time if you plan to use other preservation methods, like dehydrating, canning, or curing later down the line.

Fruits and Vegetables

You can ensure you gain the infusion of vitamins and minerals through fruits no matter the season through freezing. You can buy them already chopped and frozen and simply pack them into your freezer, or you can do the process yourself by planting or buying fresh fruits and veggies.

Freezing is not the only way to preserve fruit. If you plan on canning or dehydrating your fruits later, freezing first is not a good idea. Instead, consider turning them into jams and jellies.

Be mindful that water-heavy fruits, like cucumbers, do not freeze well.

Processed Fruits and Vegetables

Certain fresh fruits and veggies need to be processed before freezing to ensure the highest quality. Examples include apples and tomatoes. You can puree them to gain sauces, which undergo the freezing process much better.

Dairy Products

The shelf life of dairy products, like some cheeses and milk, can be increased by freezing them.

Ready to Eat Meals

Freezing is also an option for people who are not great with the stove or prefer not to have to make meals from scratch. You can freeze meals that are already ready to eat, like pizza, waffles, and premade meals.

Extras

Some foods simply do not do well being stored in a pantry (or any other space that you decide is ideal for storage). Freezing extends their shelf life without changing the flavor or texture. Examples include:
- Nut flours, like peanut flours and almond flour
- Whole wheat flour
- Bread
- Cakes
- Juice
- Eggs

Chapter 4 - The Timing of Frozen Food

There remains the question of how long you can store then safely consume frozen food. Let's break down some of these products by this standard:

1 to 2 Months
- Unbaked breads
- Cottage cheese
- Ice cream
- Raw, cracked eggs
- Yogurt
- Cooked ham
- Hotdogs
- Pizza
- Chicken nuggets
- Sausages
- Bacon
- Waffles

2 to 4 Months
- Citrus fruits
- Nuts
- Meat soups
- Meat broths
- Stew meats
- Vegetable stews
- Vegetable soups
- Cooked casseroles
- Cooked rice
- Cooked pasta
- TV dinners
- Baked breads
- Milk
- Fatty fish

- Cheesecake
- Pancakes
- Fried chicken

4 to 6 Months
- Pork chops
- Soft cheeses
- Lean fish
- Lard cheeses
- Homemade juices

6+ Months
- Baked cookies
- Pork roast
- Lamb
- Veal
- Chicken
- Turkey
- Lobster
- Crab
- Butter
- Margarine
- Vegetables
- Fruits other than citrus
- Juice concentrates
- Herbs and spices

Chapter 5 - How to Freeze Your Food

Simply sticking your food in the freezer will not do. To ensure its fresh quality, use vacuum-sealed freezer-safe bags as well as freezer-safe containers. This greatly enhances their lifespan, especially of frozen meats. Vacuum-sealed meats easily stay fresh for 12 to 16 months or even longer.

Freezing Fruit

Berries and small fruits can be placed in freezer bags and frozen. Larger fruits must be sliced. Spread the slices out of a tray, freeze for 2 hours, and then repackage into freezer bags. Whenever transferring items to a freezer bag, ensure that you have pressed out as much of the air as possible. The presence of air causes off taste, freezer burns, and the growth of microorganisms. Use a vacuum seal to get rid of the air.

Freezing Veggies

Clean, peel, and chop these items. Blanch the pieces for 2 to 3 minutes and immediately submerge in an ice water bath. Strain the pieces and pat dry with paper towels. Spread the pieces out of a tray, freeze for 2 hours, and then repackage into freezer bags.

Freezing Meat

The meat must be divided into individual portions sizes and wrapped in freezer paper or plastic wrap. Place each piece in a freezer bag and freeze.

Freezing Herbs

Finely chop or run the herbs through the food processor. Fill up the compartments of ice trays with the chopped herbs and top with olive oil or water. Freeze then pop the cubes from the tray and repackage them in freezer bags.

Chapter 6 - Freezing Techniques

It is not always possible to have access to your conventional freezer in times of crisis, but it is still possible to freeze your food under the right conditions. Freezing can be approached in several ways.

Contact Freezing

Also called conduction, contact freezing is done by placing the food between cold surfaces. This is typically used for bulk freezing, so the disadvantage here is during thawing when you might only need a small piece of the item.

Blast Freezing

This process blows cold air over the food while hot air is sucked out so that the freezing temperature is achieved.

Brine Freezing

This is an old freezing method, but it works. Brine is created from salts and placed in a tank. This is cooled, and the resulting cold air freezes the food. This process can alter the taste of the food.

Cryogenic Freezing

Liquid nitrogen is used in this method. It is sprayed over the food. Because the temperature of liquid nitrogen is less than -320 degrees F, the food freezes instantly. This is a highly costly way of freezing.

Slow and Quick Freezing

Food is considered frozen when it reaches a temperature of -64 degrees F. Slow freezing can take several hours and even days to achieve this. During the process, water might drip off the food, and this can result in nutrient loss. Brine freezing is an example of slow freezing, and it can explain why this freezing method has become outdated.

On the other hand, quick freezing allows the food to achieve a freezing temperature much quicker, sometimes even immediately, like with cryogenic freezing. This allows the food to retain its nutritional value.

Chapter 7 - Fermenting Food

Fermentation is a process that seems as old as time ... or at least as long as human beings have walked the earth. There are documents of it being used in ancient Egypt and even the Neolithic period. Many of the foods that we eat and drink, including wine, beer, and yogurt, come from the process. It is common in our everyday lives, but what is it and how can it help you survive the worst? Let's start by defining what it is.

Fermentation is the process of preserving food with the use of yeasts, special bacteria, and other microorganisms. The process is catalyzed by certain enzymes. This keeps the food from spoiling and helps preserve its nutritional value, as well.

Advantages to preserving food through fermentation include the restoration of proper bacteria in your gut. Some bacteria are good for your health. They are called probiotics, and they help improve the function of your digestive system, among many other health benefits. They are found in fermented food, like milk and yogurt.

A better-working digestive system means a stronger immune system. Your immune system controls how well your body defends itself in the face of microorganisms that are not-so-good for your health. Therefore, eating fermented food means that you will get sick less often.

Also, consuming fermented food helps lower blood pressure, which contributes to good heart health.

There is always a flip side of the coin, so the cons associated with fermenting food include an increased risk of developing gastric cancer and the possibility of food becoming contaminated.

Fermentation also changes the taste of food to one that is sharp and acidic. Whether this is a pro or a con is dependent on the individual. Some people like it, while others do not. The change in taste is a result of starches or sugars in the food being converted into acid or alcohol.

Types of Fermentation

During the process of fermentation, the end result can be only one product. This type of fermentation is called homo fermentation. It is possible for more than one product to be formed. This type of fermentation is called hetero fermentation.

Based on the number of end products, 4 types of fermentation have arisen:

Lactic Acid Fermentation

This fermentation involves the conversion of sugars, like glucose and lactose, into lactic acid. Because only one product is produced by the end, it is homo fermentation. Typical food achieved with this type of fermentation includes dairies, like cheese and yogurt, and vegetables, like kimchi and pickles.

Alcohol Fermentation

Two products are produced from this type of fermentation. These are carbon dioxide and ethanol, which are made from the conversion of glucose. It is hetero fermentation. As the name suggests, this type of fermentation is typically used to produce alcoholic products, like wine and beer.

Acetic Acid Fermentation

Also a hetero fermentation process, acetic acid fermentation yields water and acetic acid from the conversion of sugar. Vinegar is produced from this type of fermentation.

Butyric Acid Fermentation

Three end products are produced from this type of fermentation. Sugar is converted into carbon dioxide, hydrogen, and butyric acids. This is the process that gives food that has gone rancid, like butter, its pungent odor and taste.

Basic Steps to Ferment Food

Unless you are producing alcohol or vinegar, the most likely type of fermentation that you will participate in in your home is lactic acid fermentation. Vegetables are the common choice for fermentation at home. You can ferment almost any type of veggies, like carrots, green tomatoes, and cauliflower. Only veggies with tons of chlorophyll—the substance that makes leaves appear green—should not be fermented. Examples include spinach, collard greens, and kale.

You can ferment your choice of veggies alone or do a mixture of veggies. You can also include herbs and spices to customize and increase the flavor.

Fermenting veggies includes a few simple steps:

Select Your Tools

The tools of the trade for fermenters include a choice of glass mason jars, glass bowls, or a fermenting crock.

Prep Your Veggies

You have a choice of how to prepare the vegetables for fermentation:
- Grate crunchy veggies, like zucchini, to achieve a relish-like texture as the end product.
- Slice firm and soft veggies. An example of veggies that this works for include peppers. Slicing allows for keeping their shape.
- Chop larger veggies, like carrots and cauliflower, into bite-sized pieces.
- Keep them whole. Small veggies, like brussel sprouts, cucumbers, and radishes, can be kept whole for fermenting.

Prepare a Brine Solution

Combine water and salt, whey or a starter culture, to create a brine solution. The brine must be of a 2% concentration. 2 grams of salt must be used for every 100 grams of vegetables that you use.

Use filtered water to produce the brine. Tap water contains chlorine and fluoride, which kills the yeast that facilitates fermentation.

Ensure Veggies are Weighed Down

Add the veggies to the brine and ensure they remain submerged. Fermenting crocks come with a weight that keeps the veggies submerged, but you can achieve the same effect by using a small plate, cup, glass, or similar object with a bowl or mason jar. Seal the container.

Ferment!

How long your veggies take to ferment will depend on the environment that you keep them in, but the typical time is 3 days. Allow the veggies to ferment at room temperature for this period. Taste them to see if they meet your preference. If not, allow them to ferment for another 3 days. When the taste has met your preference, move the container to the refrigerator.

Best Food to Ferment

While you can ferment almost any vegetable, and a wide variety of other food, there are a few common choices that you can fall back on. This list includes:

- Kefir, which is a fermented milk item. This is packed with nutrition.
- Kombucha. This is a fermented beverage made from a mixture of honey and black tea.
- Sauerkraut, which is fermented cabbage.
- Pickles. A variety of vegetables can be pickled and cucumbers are one of the favorites.
- Miso. Soybeans, rice or barley are fermented along with koji fungus.
- Tempeh. This is made from fermenting a tempeh starter (a type of fungus) along with soybeans. It is a vegan and vegetarian favorite as it is a great source of protein.
- Natto. These are fermented soybeans. It is a favorite in Japanese culture.
- Kimchi, which is fermented cabbage along with other vegetables.
- Yogurt, which is a basic food item that can be customized to suit your taste with practices, such as adding berries.

Chapter 8 - -Dehydrating Food

The last preservation that we will discuss in this section is dehydrating.

Food dehydration is the process of drying or removing water from food. Moisture is extracted with the use of heat to inhibit the growth of microorganisms so that the food lasts longer. Historically, the process was done by placing food items to dry in the sun, but modern technology has made the process simple with the use of appliances.

There are records of dehydrating being used as a food preservation technique from prehistoric times. The first food dehydration appliance was created in 1795. There are many reasons why this method of food preservation has stuck around for so long. It is tried and true and has advantages like:

- The retention of the nutritional value of food.
- No chemicals are added.
- Saves money as there is less food wastage.
- Dried foods are easy to store because they take up less space.
- Portable, as dried food weighs less.
- Lasts longer. They last between 6 and 12 months on average, but if they are sealed in airtight containers with oxygen absorbers, they can last up to 15 years.
- Good for all emergencies, as electricity is not required to make or store them.

The possible cons of using this method of food preservation are:

- The process is not instant and can take quite some time to complete.
- The taste of the food may change.
- The food may contain excess calories.
- Can lose nutritional value over time if the food is not prepared or stored adequately.

Which Food can You Dehydrate?

The best foods to dehydrate include:
- Fruits like:
    - Apples
    - Pears
    - Peaches
    - Grapes
    - Plums
    - Cherries
    - Bananas
    - Pineapple

- Mango
    - Strawberries
    - Blueberries
    - Raspberries
    - Blackberries
    - Cranberries
    - Oranges
    - Lemons
- Vegetables like:
    - Tomatoes
    - Celery
    - Kale
    - Onions
    - Bell Peppers
    - Garlic
    - Mushrooms
    - Pumpkin
    - Green beans
    - Corn
    - Potatoes
    - Sweet potatoes
    - Broccoli
    - Zucchini
    - Squash
    - Carrots
- Meats like:
    - Beef
    - Turkey
    - Chicken
    - Fish
    - Deli meats
    - Canned meats
- Jams
- Yogurt
- Sauces like:

- BBQ sauce
- Pizza sauce
- Tomato sauce
- Ketchup
- Mustard
- Alfredo sauce
- Herbs like:
  - Rosemary
  - Thyme
  - Basil
  - Oregano
  - Mint
  - Sage
- Syrups like:
  - Maple syrup
  - Molasses
  - Agave syrup
  - Corn syrup
- Honey

The Dehydrating Process

So, how do you dehydrate your choice of food? Let's get right into the details of that now!

The Tools Needed

- An electric dehydrator
- Dehydrating recipe
- Kitchen utensils to prepare food items for dehydration
- Airtight and moisture-resistant storage containers and bags with sealable lids. Containers and lids must be washed, rinsed, and dried before use. Bags should be new and uncontaminated.

With your tools gathered and your dehydration recipe in mind, you can move on to the act of drying out your food.

5 Steps to Perfectly Dehydrated Food

1. Prep your ingredients for dehydration according to your recipe instructions. For example, many fruits and veggies need to be chopped, sliced, or blanched before they are dried. These processes shorten the drying time and ensure your food has the longest shelf life.

    Meats (and fruits and veggies if you want to add extra flavor) need to be seasoned according to your recipe or your preference.

    You can also preserve the color of your food, fruits, and veggies especially by soaking the sliced and chopped pieces in an acidic solution, like vitamin C tablets or lemon juice, before dehydrating them. Alternatively, you can spray the pieces with the acidic solution with a spray bottle instead of soaking them. Luckily, this does not change the flavor.

2. Follow the manufacturer's instructions for your electric dehydrator to dehydrate your food.
3. Package your dried food in vacuumed sealed bags, containers, or canning jars.
4. Label the packaged food with the date and name of the food items.
5. Store the dried food in a dry, dark place with a temperature between 50 and 70 degrees F.

    Remember to check this storage area and items regularly for the growth of mold and the presence of moisture. If the ideal conditions of your storage space change, dispose of the dried food.

Book 4:
The Ultimate Prepper's Food List

A trip (or several) to the grocery store is definitely needed as you prepare an adequate supply of food that will allow you to survive for at least 2 weeks in the case of an emergency. An adequately stocked pantry consists of the following groups of products:

- Grains
- Beans and Legumes
- Fats
- Meats and proteins
- Spices

As promised earlier, the aim of this book is to make the process of preparing for survival as easy as possible, so below you will find a comprehensive list of products that you can take with you to the grocery store to stock up.

Grains

Grains have a long shelf life and can be used as the base to prepare a variety of dishes. Some of the items that will be listed below have a shelf life of up to 20 years! They include:

- Rice. You can get several varieties of rice, like basmati, short grain, white, etc.

- Wheat berries
- Dried corn
- Popcorn
- Rolled oats
- Oatmeal
- Cornmeal
- All-purpose flour
- Crackers
- Pancake mixes
- Cake flour
- Pasta
- Quinoa
- Rye
- Barley
- Buckwheat
- Spelt
- Flax
- Millet
- Instant grits
- Kamut
- Instant mashed potatoes
- Potato flakes
- Potato flour
- Special bake wheat

Grains that should not be stored include pearl barley and pot barley. Brown rice normally has a short shelf life of 4 to 6 months but this can be extended by cooking and then dehydrating it. This creates instant brown rice that can be stored almost indefinitely.

Both pearl and pot barley are highly processed and the outer hull is removed. As such, the barley is unprotected and breaks during storage. These two items also have shorter than needed shelf lives. Whole wheat flour also has a short shelf life.

To ensure that the grains that you do buy last as long as possible, use oxygen absorbers, food storage bags, vacuum or heat sealer, and food-grade buckets to keep them fresh. Start by pouring the grains into storage bags. Add an oxygen absorber into each bag. Push out any air from the bag and use a vacuum or heat sealer to seal the bag. Lastly, add the sealed bags to the food-grade bucket and seal. Place these in a cool area.

Beans and Legumes

These are a great source of protein and can be stored for a long time. They also allow for adding variety and flavor to meals. Possible additions to this list include:

- Pinto beans
- Black beans
- Black-eye peas
- Navy beans
- Cannellini beans
- Soybeans (edamame)
- Kidney beans
- Green peas
- Chickpeas (garbanzo beans)
- Lima beans
- Black-eyed peas
- White beans
- Lentils
- Split peas
- Cranberry beans (Roman beans)
- Pink beans
- Fava beans

Stored properly, some of these items can last up to 30 years. Follow the same instructions stated for storing grains to keep your beans and legumes fresh for as long as possible.

Fats

Fats play several roles in a survivalist's pantry. They provide healthy nutrition, as long as they are used in moderation and are of the unsaturated variety. They help you feel full faster so that you eat less. They can aid the cooking process by allowing stir-frying and sautéing. They also have a great shelf life, as they tend to last between 1 and 2 years. Examples of healthy fats that can be placed in your pantry for emergencies include:

- Nut butters, like peanut butter, almond butter, and cashew butter
- Canola oil
- Olive oil
- Coconut oil
- Soy oil

- Corn oil
- Sunflower oil
- Avocado oil
- Sesame oil
- Safflower oil
- Palm oil
- Walnut oil

Meats and Proteins

The best options for these to ensure long shelf life are canned varieties. Dry-cured meat products are also options that have longer than usual shelf lives.

You are not limited to just meats and poultry to get the infusion of protein into your diet. There are also vegan and vegetarian options to keep your diet well-rounded.

Options in this category include:
- Canned salmon
- Textured vegetable protein (TVP)
- Canned sardines
- Canned chicken
- Canned tuna
- Spam
- Vienna sausages
- Textured vegetable protein
- Canned smoked mussels
- Canned anchovies
- Dry-cured bacon
- Whole country ham
- Canned beef
- Canned mackerel
- Luncheon meat
- Corned beef
- Canned turkey

Spices

Add variety and flavor to your dishes with spices. They allow you to take the monotony out of eating if you have to use the same ingredient constantly.

The top items on this list are absolute must-haves:
- Salt
- Granulated sugar
- Honey
- White vinegar

Note that if your honey crystallizes during storage, simply soak the container in warm water to regain the fluid texture.

The next few items are optional and depend on your preferences. Simply remove and add desired items to this list:
- Apple cider vinegar
- Rice wine vinegar
- Soy sauce
- Black peppercorns
- Cinnamon sticks
- Ground cinnamon
- Dried mustard
- Ground ginger
- Dried rosemary
- Chicken bouillon
- Garlic powder
- Italian seasoning
- Garam masala
- Chili powder
- Paprika
- Cumin
- Cayenne pepper
- Curry bars
- Coriander

Condiments

Another way to give your taste buds something to look forward to, even under strenuous conditions, is the use of condiments.

- Mayonnaise
- Mustard
- Pickle relish
- Soy sauce
- Tabasco sauce
- Worcestershire sauce

Fruits and Vegetables

Don't think that you have to give up on fruits and vegetables during times of crisis. You simply have to get creative with the way that they are stored. Fruits can be obtained in canned, freeze-dried, dried, dehydrated, jammed, jellied, and sauced versions. Examples of fruits that you can stock up on include:

- Canned peaches
- Canned pineapples
- Prunes
- Canned mango
- Canned pears
- Raisins
- Dried apricots
- dried berries, like blueberries and cranberries
- Dried figs
- Dried dates
- Applesauce
- Banana chips
- Dehydrated apples
- Freeze-dried pears
- Freeze-dried sliced strawberries
- Cherry jam
- Apricot jelly

Veggies can typically be found in the canned variety in prepper panties. Examples of such items include:

- Spinach

- Corn
- Mushrooms
- Carrots
- Asparagus
- Mixed vegetables
- Tomatoes
- Olives
- Pumpkin
- Beets

The items listed above are only a short snippet of what you can add to your pantry. This list is entirely dependent on you. Being in a crisis does not mean that your taste buds or your stomach have to suffer. Not if you are prepared.

In the next part of this book, you will gain extra knowledge in the preparation of an adequate food supply for any survival situation with a guide to stocking up on canned food.

Book 5:
Stocking Up on Canned Food

Chapter 1 - The Preparation

Canning is the heat processing of preserving food, particularly fruits and vegetables, in sealed, airtight containers, like mason jars. Canning was once thought to be the domain where grandmothers reside, but the rising popularity of canning has shown that anyone and everyone can enjoy the pleasure of the practice.

Why is canning becoming such a trending application, especially among preppers? It's because all the advantages are being exposed. For one, the range of food that can be canned is quite extensive. In summer weather, you can take advantage of the items that grow in abundance, like berries, plums, and sun-kissed tomatoes. Canned food can actually ensure you put more fruits and vegetables into your diet, especially since you can customize the flavor to suit your palate. Canning also saves you freezer space for items that are better frozen.

After canning, you can enjoy the food at any time, including in the middle of winter. Preppers do not have to miss out on their favorite food in an emergency since, on average, home-canned goods last up to 18 months or longer. Even better is that you are not limited to canning just fruits and veggies. Additional items that can be canned in the comfort of your home include:

- Meats, like dried jerky, pot roasts, and poultry.
- Fish and seafood
- Burger patties
- Bacon
- Hot dogs
- Condiments, like relish, sauces, and pickles
- Jams, curds, and marmalades
- Dairies, like cheese and butter
- Soups
- Pasta
- Cereal

Building on the pros that we have listed for canning so far, canned food can be just as nutritious as fresh food.

Foods are canned with the use of heat. Many people worry that this can destroy the nutritional value of foods, but the truth is that it does not happen on such a significant value that the food becomes innutritious.

Canning is often done immediately after fruits and vegetables have just been harvested, which should be at the peak of their nutritional value. Canning the items at that time means you will still have plenty of nutrition available after the process is complete. The only concern is that the canning process may break down water-soluble vitamins, like vitamin B and vitamin C, during the process. However, you can make up for this in other ways, such as taking and stocking up on supplements. You can also use other preservation methods for food that contain high amounts of these nutrients.

It is also a point to note that the heating process in canning food can actually increase the antioxidant content of food. Antioxidants are nutritional substances that help prevent and delay damage to the body's cells. They also help improve your brain health and function, as well as your heart health and many other benefits. They are often found in brightly colored fruits and vegetables, like berries and pomegranates.

Canning is carving a way for itself as a great method of preserving found in this age of uncertainty in human history. You can adopt the practice with ease, not to be on the trending end of things, but to gain another method of ensuring yours, and your family's, survival during any event.

This chapter gives you the breakdown of how to can easily at home, how to ensure your food remains safe to consume as you do so, and even a few easy recipes to get you started.

Chapter 2 - Intro to Canned Food

At this point, you might be wondering why can your own food instead of just buying canned food at the store? After all, it is more convenient and would save you time to just take things off the grocery shelf and place them in your chosen storage area. Only you can choose what works best for you and your home, but this book gives you the facts so that you can make an informed choice. So, let's weigh home-canning against buying canned food.

The first thing we will consider is the cost. Upfront, it looks like store-bought canned food is the clear winner. Canning at home requires that you get special containers and canners. You *need* to get these items. There is also the cost of the raw ingredients, like the fruits and veggies. Additionally, if you own your own garden, there is the time and cost of growing these items.

If you think about getting the cheapest canned food that you can source at the supermarket, it can seem like that route is cheaper, but wait a minute and look at the ingredients in these canned foods. Unless these cans specifically say these canned foods are 100% organic, you will likely find ingredients like GMOs, high fructose syrup, preservatives, and lots of sugar listed on these canned foods. Eating these items erodes your health. Compared to all these other costs, I would say that your health is the one that counts most. Also, after the initial buying of the containers and equipment, you're all set in that regard when you can at home.

There is also the consideration of time. Most people can food in bulk, so their canned goods last them over the long-term since it is not a one-off use. Canning can take time. Those times vary based on the exact method of canning used, the food being canned, and the processing times for these foods. When thinking about the amount of time spent going to and from the supermarket and handpicking items, is buying canned food the time-saving activity that you think it is? Those times can rack up when you consider throwing out expired items and having to replace them with fresh ones.

So, is it worth it to can your own food? The answer to that is absolutely. Canning allows you to take complete control of your health, pocket, and any dependence that you might have on what is stocked on supermarket shelves. Your pantry (or any other food storage area) can become your personal grocery store with a stock of all types of canned food. It can save you cooking time, as the foods are partially or fully cooked. Therefore, a cooked meal can be on your table within minutes.

A decision is before you—to can your own food or not. I hope that you have decided on the former. Not only is canning a great way of preserving your food in case of emergencies, but it is also a fun hobby. Keep on reading to gain all the details you need to get started today.

Chapter 3 - Canning Your Own Food

In general, canning involves three main steps:

Processing

It would be nice if you could simply take food as is and simply throw it into jars, but it does not work out so easily. Instead, you need to prep the food for the process. The first thing that must be done is to clean the food where it is necessary. Fruits and vegetables must be washed, rinsed, and dried. Stems must be removed, where it applies. Also, remove any bruises and blemishes from the food.

Once the food is cleaned, you can proceed to pitting, slicing, chopping, boning, and any other preparation process that your canning recipe dictates.

Just like with dehydrating food, you can infuse flavor and prevent darkening during the preparation process. Herbs and spices can be used to add and customize the flavor. Acidic solutions can be used to prevent darkening.

Sealing

After processing, the food must be placed in sealable jars.

Heating

The sealed jars are heated to lengthen the shelf life of the food and kill any microorganism that might pose a risk to your health.

Chapter 4 – The Methods of Canning

You are not limited to one method of canning. There are several to choose from to make the process as comfortable and affordable as possible for you.

The Boiling Water Bath Method

This method of canning also goes by the name of "hot water canning" or "boiling water bath." To achieve great quality end products, all you have to do is put your processed food into jars then place these jars into a pot of boiling water for 10 minutes or more. The exact time will be based on the canning recipe's instructions. The process of heating is done on a stovetop. Do not try to can in ovens, dishwashers, or microwaves. These are not safe practices.

Water bath canning is only appropriate for vegetables that are high in acidity. Some examples of high-acidity produce include tomatoes, cucumbers, berries, and sauerkraut. As a result of this, water bath canning is great for making items like pickled veggies, jellies, and jams due to their naturally high acidity. I love making crushed tomatoes, strawberry jam, and crunchy dill pickles using water baths.

Water bath canning is not appropriate for low acidity produce like corn, poultry, seafood, and meats, because they require higher temperatures not achieved by simply boiling water. The boiling point for water is 212 degrees F while the latter items listed require a higher temperature of 240 degrees F, or higher, to raise the heat inside the jars enough to achieve safe canning.

The items required to achieve this method of canning include:
- A boiling water canner, which is a deep pot, typically made of aluminum. The canner needs a fitted lid for covering to sustain the internal temperature. Also, it needs to be deep enough to submerge the canning jars at least 1 inch above the tops. The bottom of the canner needs to be flat, as well. If you do not have a boiling water canner, you can substitute this with a stock pot with similar features.
- A rack to fit inside of the canner or stock pot so that the jars do not sit directly on the bottom of the canner. Direct contact will cause the jars to crack.
- Canning jars.
- Metal, rust-free bands to fit around the jars to keep them sealed.
- Single-use metal bands to fit on the jars. These are the safest, most hygienic option. However, reusable lids can be used.
- A canning funnel to keep your food from spilling while you are filling up the jars.
- A stainless-steel(or plastic) ladle for filling up the canning jars.
- A jar lifter to remove the jars from the canner.
- A strainer to remove skin, seeds, or pulp where it applies to the recipe.

The Pressure Canner Method

As the name suggests, this method of home canning requires the use of a pressure canner. Not to be confused with pressure cooking, pressure canning uses special equipment to process food at high temperatures to ensure that the food has a longer shelf life. This pressure canner is what allows the achievement of the higher temperature needed to preserve items, like meat and poultry.

Pressure is typically used to preserve low acidic food. Vegetables that fit this criterion include asparagus, lima beans, carrots, onions, peas, pumpkin, corn, winter squash, and mushrooms. Low acidic fruits include watermelon and cantaloupe. All other fruits are highly acidic.

Unlike water bath canning, which does not require the purchase of any specialized equipment, with pressure canning, you need to invest in a pressure canner. This cost can run you upward of $100. Apart from purchasing a pressure canner, the typical canning equipment listed above is used for the process. Simply follow the instructions outlined in your recipe.

The Atmospheric Steam Canner Method

This canning method is another one meant for highly acidic food. That means no canning of low acidity produce or other food. Most fruits (apples, cherries, peaches, etc.), pickled veggies, jellies, and jams are on the list of approved items, though. Water bath canning was the dominating process for canning high acidic food for a long time until atmospheric steam canning entered the arena. Just like with water bath canning, the food is canned with a temperature achievement of 212 degrees F. 2 more conditions must be met to use this method of canning safely:

The canning jars must be heated before they are placed in the heater. This can be done by filling them with hot water or using a hot rack.

The processing time must be increased at high elevations.

You do not need specialized equipment for creating your own steam canner at home. You can set one up with pans you already have. Use a shallow pan at the bottom. Fit this with a rack and place the jars over it. Place a deep lid or a deep pan over to trap the steam generated by boiling the water in the shallow pan. Alternatively, you can purchase a steam canner.

This process is done on a stovetop, as well. Steam canning uses a lot less water to achieve the same results as water bath canning. Only use this method of canning for water bath canning recipes that can be processed in less than 45 minutes.

The General Canning Steps

No matter the method of canning you choose, there are a few general rules you must follow to ensure the end product is safe and tasty. These rules are:

- Locate a recipe.
- Gather your ingredients.
- Process your ingredients and follow the recipe.
- Prepare your canning jars, containers, and pots.
- Prepare the canning lids.
- Fill the prepared containers with the food and seal the containers.
- Start the timer and can your food.
- Check the seal after the canning process is over and the containers have cooled.
- Store the canned food in a cool, dry, dark space.

Chapter 5 – Safety and Maintenance

As mentioned before, one of the possible downsides of home canning is the food may lose its nutritional value over time. Therefore, the high-quality product with great taste and tons of nutrients that you started off with may not be what you eat weeks later, even if the food is still safely edible. You do not have to suffer that heartache (and you will definitely feel a little sore in the chest after putting in all that effort only to eat a subpar product). The way you can avoid this from happening is to ensure you safely store your canned (and other stored food) as well as maintain that storage. You cannot just set it down and forget it. But with proper planning and maintenance, you can set it aside and only have to check on it periodically.

Proper storage starts even before you can a single veggie. It starts with your planning, which is broken down into the following steps:

Take Stock

Know what you already have and what you would like to have on hand. This will allow you to create a grocery list of all the items you need to stock up on.

Set a Budget

Give yourself a limit to spend, or you will go off on a tangent. Being a prepper does not mean you have to break the bank to be prepared.

Buy Slowly and for Long-Term

Prepping and canning is a continuous process. Therefore, do not worry about getting everything you need in one day. Buy what you need now by focusing on must-haves and the longest storage. Then slowly rotate and swap items as time goes by and when you perhaps need to change.

Get Things on Sale

This is a great way to save. Look out for deals and schedule shopping based on these circumstances. Also, don't be afraid of the dollar store.

Pantry Rotation

Rotating the items in your pantry is an important step in ensuring your food, canned and otherwise, is as fresh as possible when you do indulge in them. Pantry rotation refers to the act of eating the oldest food in your pantry first. Practicing pantry rotation relies on what people in the restaurant and other food industries call the first-in-first-out system. There are many benefits to adopting this as *your* practice. Such benefits include:

- Ensuring that you always have fresh food on hand.
- Aiding protecting you from food spoilage, and thus wastage.
- Prompting for inspection for pest infestation.
- Ensuring regular inventory of food stock is taken.

So, how do you go about rotating your pantry? It's not complicated. Here are the steps:

- Mark and date everything that you prep yourself before you give them a place in your pantry.
- Ensure that you have the expiration dates of everything. Luckily, store-bought items have this marked on them, but you need to figure this out with the items that you preserve yourself. I will provide a few tips on this in the next section. Mark this on the item, as well.
- Follow the first in, first out concept. Place the items that will expire soonest in the front of your pantry so that you do not have to search for the oldest items with every visit to the pantry. Place the oldest items in the front every time you stock up your food storage.
- Get rid of any item that shows signs of spoilage or damage with every pantry inspection. Inspections should also consist of looking for pests.

Make rotating your pantry easier by stocking stackable food items. How your pantry is organized plays a big role in how easily you can access the items you place there. Having all the shelves in the world in your pantry will not help you if your food items are falling all over each other. Standardize the storage containers and jars you buy so they fit neatly one on top of the other.

Also, when purchasing and preserving food, consider the capacity you have to store food and how quickly you will consume these items. Ensure these two factors match up so that you do not run out of food too quickly and never stock too much and end up with wasted products since you could not consume them before they went bad.

Lastly, ensure that the conditions remain optimal for food storage. As a gentle reminder, these conditions include the presence (or lack thereof) of oxygen, light, heat, moisture, and pests.

How Long Does Home Canned Food Last?

Many factors will affect the shelf life of your home-canned food. For example, high temperatures and the rusting and corrosion of container components will eat away at that time. Time is the only consistent factor that will act on any food item no matter how well preserved and stored it is. Therefore, in addition to maintaining the storage conditions of your canned food, you must determine the expiration date of these items.

Before we get to how to determine this, we need to address a critical issue. Expiration dates do not mean that a food item is automatically bad for your health if you consume it on or past that date. Instead, the expiration date states the date when the food is at its best quality and still has the highest nutritional value. Time changes the taste, texture, and nutritional value of foods, so it is best to consume them as close to the manufacture date, or original date of preservation, as possible.

When stored optimally, home-canned goods tend to expire within these periods:
- High acidic food – 1- to 1.5-year shelf life. Must be refrigerated after opening and consumed within 7 days.
- Low acidic food – 2- to 5-year shelf life. Must be refrigerated after opening and consumed within 4 days.
- Ham – 2- to 5-year shelf life. Must be refrigerated after opening and consumed within 4 days.

Based on these values, when canning at home, you can assume it is safe to consume properly canned products within 1 year and within 4 days after opening and refrigerating. Even if you do not detect any signs of spoilage, boil high acidic food for 10 minutes before eating them and low acidity food for 20 minutes before eating them.

Book 6:
The Best Canned Food Recipes

It would not do you justice to not give you a few canning recipes to ensure a great start to the craft. Therefore, I have compiled some of the best (and beginner-friendly) recipes in this section. Not only will I provide these recipes, but I will also list which canning method is best for that food item and why that particular recipe has earned a place in your pantry.

Beef Stew

This is a basic but handy way of having a hot meal ready within minutes. Streamline the canning process by prepping the beef and vegetables beforehand. Your typical beef stew recipe consists of cubed beef, potatoes that have been peeled and cubed, and peeled and sliced veggies, like onions and carrots. You can, of course, customize the specific ingredients that fit your taste.

This recipe uses a pressure canner as this is a meat recipe.

Prep: 35 Minutes | Canning Time: 1 Hour 30 Minutes | Makes: 8 Servings

INGREDIENTS

- 1 lb. beef chuck, cut into 1 inch piece
- 1 medium yellow onion, chopped into 1 inch chunk
- 3 garlic cloves, minced
- 1 carrot, chopped
- 2 potatoes, chopped
- 4 cups low-sodium beef broth
- 1 tbsp Italian seasoning
- ½ tsp salt

DIRECTIONS

1. Prepare 8 canning jars (quarts) by filling them with hot (180 degrees F) water.
2. Add 3 inches of water (or as recommended by the canner's manufacturer manual) to the pressure canner and bring to a simmer.
3. Fill the preheated jars one at a time with the processed food items, starting with the chopped beef and ending with the Italian seasoning and salt.
4. Top with the beef broth. Leave 1 inch of headspace at the top of the jar. Use a rubber spatula to release any trapped air from between the items in the jar. Repeat until all the jars have been filled.
5. Wipe the rims of each jar with a clean, damp cloth to remove any food residue.
6. Close the jars with the accompanying lids by allowing the sealing compound to contact the rims of the jars. Apply a band around each rim until they form a fingertip-tight fit.
7. Place the jars in the canner.
8. Apply the canner lid and leave the vent pipe open. Adjust the heat to medium-high and allow steam to escape from the vent pipe until the steam comes in a constant flow. This should take around 10 minutes.
9. Close the canner's vent as described by the manufacturer manual or using a weight.
10. Allow the cans to process at constant pressure for 90 minutes.
11. Turn off the heat and allow the pressure to come down slowly. This will take approximately 30 to 45 minutes.
12. When the pressure is down to zero, remove the weight and allow the jars to sit for 10 minutes.
13. Remove the jars from the canner and set them on the counter. Do not tip the jars. Ensure that they remain level and leave them undisturbed for 12 to 24 hours so that they seal completely.
14. Before storing the cans, remove the bands, check the seals, and wipe down the jars. If any of the jars failed during the canning process, refrigerate them and consume the contents within 24 hours.
15. Label and date the jars. Store well.

Pork Beans

As good as the beans found on any grocery shelf, this recipe is great served by itself or accompanied by side dishes. It is also great for vegetarians and vegans.

For this canning recipe, you need to use a pressure canner.

Prep: 25 Minutes | Canning Time: 1 Hour 30 Minutes | Makes: 6 Servings

INGREDIENTS
- 3 cups navy beans, rinsed, and sorted
- ⅓ cup brown sugar
- ½ tbsp yellow mustard
- 2 tbsp honey
- 2 cups tomato sauce
- 3 cups water
- 1 tbsp salt
- ½ cup yellow onion, chopped
- 6 pieces bacon

DIRECTIONS
1. Prepare 6 canning jars (quarts) by filling them with hot (180 degrees F) water.
2. Add 3" of water (or as recommended by the canner's manufacturer manual) to the pressure canner and bring to a simmer.
3. Create a sauce by combining the honey, brown sugar, tomato sauce, water, and mustard in a saucepan over medium heat on a stovetop. Bring to a boil while stirring occasionally. Turn off the heat.
4. Fill the preheated jars one at a time. Place ½ cup of the navy beans at the bottom of each jar. Next, layer each jar with onions and a piece of bacon.
5. Ladle the sauce equally on top of the contents of each jar.
6. Add boiling water to each jar until 1 inch of headspace is left.
7. Wipe the rims of each jar with a clean, damp cloth to remove any food residue.
8. Repeat Steps 6 to 15 of the previous recipe.

Canned Meat

Perhaps you do not have a pressure canner and would still like to can meat items. Typically, it is discouraged, as canning meat requires a temperature above 240 degrees F. Typically, the maximum temperature achieved with water bath canning is 212 degrees F. Heat-resistant bacteria will not be killed off under these conditions. Such bacteria thrive in low acidic environments, conditions where there is no oxygen and at room temperature. So, how do you kill these bacteria in a water bath? The solution is to raise the temperature to at least 240 degrees F for at least 75 minutes.

This can be achieved by using an instant pot while practicing the water bath canning method. Ensure that the instant pot that you use displays temperature and pressure readings.

This section features two recipes: one that allows you to can meat using a water bath and, of course, the more conventional method of using a pressure canner.

Bath Water Canned Version

Prep: 15 Minutes | Canning Time: 1 Hour 15 Minutes | Makes: 4 Servings

INGREDIENTS
- 2 lbs. meat, such as beef, lamb, pork, or wild game, like elk or venison, chopped into 1" pieces
- Desired seasonings
- Salt and pepper to taste

DIRECTIONS
1. Season the meat with the desired seasoning, salt and pepper. Place in a bowl, cover with plastic wrap, and allow to marinate for at least 1 hour.
2. Place 4 clean canning jars into the rack in the instant pot and add 3 cups of water. Do not include the lids. Press "Canning" on the instant pot and sterilize the jars on low pressure for a minimum of 10 minutes.
3. Remove the jars from the instant pot with a can lifter and place the seasoned meat into each. Do not pack the meat tightly and do not add any extra liquid, as the meat will release sufficiently.
4. Wipe the rims of each jar with a clean, damp cloth to remove any food residue.
5. Close the jars with the accompanying lids by allowing the sealing compound to contact the rims of the jars. Apply a band around each rim until they form a fingertip-tight fit.
6. Place the jars back in the instant pot.
7. Add more water to the instant pot so that the level is quarter way up the sides of the jars.
8. Set the following conditions for the instant pot:
    - Timer - 75 minutes
    - Pressure - Max
    - Venting - Normal
    - Setting - Canning

9. Press "Start."
10. Allow the timer to run for 75 minutes.
11. Allow the instant pot to naturally release the pressure when the time is up. This will take about an hour.
12. Remove the cans from the instant pot and set them on the counter.
13. Label and date the jars. Store well.

Pressure Canned Version

Prep: 15 Minutes | Canning Time: 1 Hour 30 Minutes | Makes: 4 Servings

INGREDIENTS

- 2 lbs. meat, such as beef, lamb, pork, or wild game, like elk or venison, chopped into 1 inch pieces
- Desired seasonings
- Salt and pepper to taste

DIRECTIONS

1. Season the meat with the desired seasoning, salt and pepper. Place in a bowl, cover with plastic wrap, and allow to marinate for at least 1 hour.
2. Prepare 4 canning jars (quarts) by filling them with hot (180 degrees F) water.
3. Add 3 inches of water (or as recommended by the canner's manufacturer manual) to the pressure canner and bring to a simmer.
4. Fill the preheated jars one at a time with the processed meat. Do not pack the meat tightly and do not add any extra liquid as the meat will release sufficiently.
5. Wipe the rims of each jar with a clean, damp cloth to remove any food residue.
6. Close the jars with the accompanying lids by allowing the sealing compound to contact the rims of the jars. Apply a band around each rim until they form a fingertip-tight fit.
7. Place the jars in the canner.
8. Repeat Steps 8 to 15 of the canned *Beef Stew* recipe.

Canned Fruits and Vegetables

As mentioned before, going without your fruits and veggies is not an absolute condition, no matter how dire the times. All it takes is a little time and preparation, and you can stock up on these items so that you can gain the valuable nutrients that they provide. Below, you will find recipes for canning a few of the most popular produce items.

Tomatoes

Canning tomatoes allows you to prepare a variety of soups, spaghetti sauce, and salsa. This section will provide you with two recipes: one for raw packing tomatoes and another to create tomato sauce. Both of these recipes will be using the water bath canning method. The pressure canning method can also be used, as it shortens the canning time.

Raw Pack Version

Prep: 20 Minutes | Canning Time: 1 Hour 25 Minutes | Makes: 8 Servings

INGREDIENTS
- 12 lbs. tomatoes
- 4 tbsp lemon juice
- 4 tsp salt

DIRECTIONS
1. Wash 4 canning jars (quarts) with soapy water and rinse with hot water. Fill the water bath canner with water and bring it to a boil. Put the washed jars into the boiling water, ensuring that they are submerged. Boil for 10 minutes to sterilize the jars. Turn off the heat but do not remove the jars from the canning until you are ready to fill them with your food item. If you allow the jars to cool, they will break while you are filling them with hot food items.
2. Add washed tomatoes to boiling water and cook for 30 to 60 seconds or until the tomato skins split.
3. Remove the tomatoes and immediately drop them into a bowl of cold water to stop the cooking process.
4. Slip the skins off the tomatoes.
5. Quarter the tomatoes with a paring knife and add to a bowl.
6. Add lemon juice and salt and lightly mix.
7. Place the tomatoes into the warm jars.
8. Press the tomatoes down into the jars so that all spaces are filled and the tomatoes are lightly crushed to release some of the juice. Leave ½ inch headspace in each jar.
9. Remove any air bubbles.
10. Wipe the rims of each jar with a clean, damp cloth to remove any food residue.
11. Close the jars with the accompanying lids by allowing the sealing compound to contact the rims of the jars. Apply a band around each rim until they form a fingertip-tight fit.
12. Replace the jars in the warm canner. Top the canner with warm water if required to ensure that all the jars are submerged. Cover the pot with a lid.

13. Bring the canner to a boil and allow the jars to process for 85 minutes.
14. Turn off the heat and allow the canner to rest for 5 minutes with jars submerged in the water.
15. Lift the jars enough so that they are not submerged in the water and allow them to rest for 5 minutes.
16. Remove the jars from the canner and place them on the countertop. Leave them undisturbed for at least 12 hours so that they seal completely.
17. Before storing the cans, remove the bands, check the seals, and wipe down the jars. If any of the jars failed during the canning process, refrigerate and consume the contents within 24 hours.
18. Label and date the jars. Store well.

Tomato Sauce Version

Prep: 20 Minutes | Canning Time: 1 Hour 25 Minutes | Makes: 8 Servings

INGREDIENTS
- 12 lbs. tomatoes
- 4 tbsp lemon juice
- 4 tsp salt

DIRECTIONS
1. Sterilize the jars using the same methodology stated in step 1 of the *Raw Packing Version* recipe to create canned tomatoes.
2. Add washed tomatoes to boiling water and cook for 30 to 60 seconds or until the tomato skins split.
3. Remove the tomatoes and immediately drop them into a bowl of cold water to stop the cooking process.
4. Slip the skins off the tomatoes.
5. Quarter the tomatoes with a paring knife and add to a saucepan.
6. Add the lemon juice and salt and lightly mix.
7. Place the mixture in a blender and process to a smooth consistency.
8. Divide the tomato sauce equally and place it in the warm canning jars.
9. Remove any air bubbles.
10. Wipe the rims of each jar with a clean, damp cloth to remove any food residue.
11. Repeat Steps 11 to 18 of the *Raw Packing Version* recipe.

Green Beans

This recipe relies on the pressure canning method. Green beans can be canned as a hot pack (cooked) or a cold (or raw) pack (uncooked). Recipes for both canning methods are provided below.

Hot Pack Version

Prep: 15 Minutes | Canning Time: 25 Minutes | Makes: 10 Servings

INGREDIENTS

- 15 lbs. green beans, snapped
- 1 tsp salt

DIRECTIONS

1. Prepare 10 canning jars (quarts) by filling them with hot (180 degrees F) water.
2. Add 3 inches of water (or as recommended by the canner's manufacturer manual) to the pressure canner and bring to a simmer.
3. Boil the snapped beans for 5 minutes.
4. Drain the beans and pack them into the jars. Do not pack tightly.
5. Cover the beans with clean, boiling water, leaving 1 inch of headspace in each jar.
6. Add salt to each jar.
7. Wipe the rims of each jar with a clean, damp cloth to remove any food residue.
8. Close the jars with the accompanying lids by allowing the sealing compound to contact the rims of the jars. Apply a band around each rim until they form a fingertip-tight fit.
9. Place the jars in the canner.
10. Apply the canner lid and leave the vent pipe open. Adjust the heat to medium-high and allow steam to escape from the vent pipe until the steam comes in a constant flow.
11. Close the canner's vent as described by the manufacturer manual or using a weight.
12. Allow the jars to process at constant pressure for 25 minutes.
13. Turn off the heat and allow the pressure to come down slowly.
14. When the pressure is down to zero, remove the weight and allow the cans to sit for 10 minutes.
15. Remove the cans from the canner and set them on the counter. Do not tip the jars. Ensure that they remain level and leave them undisturbed for 12 hours.
16. Before storing the cans, remove the bands, check the seals, and wipe down the jars. If any of the jars failed during the canning process, refrigerate them and consume the contents within 24 hours.
17. Label and date the jars. Store well.

Cold Pack Version

Prep: 10 Minutes | Canning Time: 25 Minutes | Makes: 10 Servings

INGREDIENTS
- 15 lbs. green beans, snapped
- 1 tsp salt

DIRECTIONS
1. Prepare 10 canning jars (quarts) by filling them with hot (180 degrees F) water.
2. Add 3" of water (or as recommended by the canner's manufacturer manual) to the pressure canner and bring to a simmer.
3. Pack the snapped beans into the jars. Do not pack tightly.
4. Cover the beans with clean, boiling water, leaving 1 inch of headspace in each jar.
5. Add salt to each jar.
6. Wipe the rims of each jar with a clean, damp cloth to remove any food residue.
7. Repeat Steps 8 to 17 of the previous recipe.

Beets

Beets are one of those veggies that people either love or hate. If you are a lover of beets, then this recipe is definitely the one for you.

Canned beets can be used to create a variety of delicious food, including smoothies and soups. They can be used to jazz up sauces, dressings, and jams. They can even be added to baked goods, like cakes and muffins, to add extra decadence.

Beets are classified as low acidic food. Therefore, the best method for canning them is with a pressure canner. As such, the recipe below follows that guideline.

Prep: 50 Minutes | Canning Time: 35 Minutes | Makes: 20 Servings

INGREDIENTS
- 10 lbs. beets
- 1 tsp salt

DIRECTIONS
1. Prepare the jars as stated in previous pressure canning recipes.
2. Cut the stems of the beets a minimum of 2 inches and keep the taproot to maintain as much of the color of the vegetable.
3. Boil the beets for about 45 minutes or until they are tender.
4. Immediately submerge the beets in cold water to stop the cooking process.

5. Remove the taproots, stems, and skins of the beets.
6. Chop the beets into bite-sized pieces and add them to the jars.
7. Add clean, boiling water to the jars, leaving 1 inch of headspace in each.
8. Add salt to each jar.
9. Wipe the rims of each jar with a clean, damp cloth to remove any food residue.
10. Close the jars with the accompanying lids by allowing the sealing compound to contact the rims of the jars. Apply a band around each rim until they form a fingertip-tight fit.
11. Place the jars in the canner.
12. Proceed as usual with previous pressure canning recipes, leaving the jars in the canner for 35 minutes.

Raw Pack Corn

You can also create hot-pack, home-canned corn by simply boiling the corn for 5 minutes before adding it to the jars. The process that will be used to can the corn in these recipes will be pressure canning.

Prep: 5 Minutes | Canning Time: 1 Hour 25 Minutes | Makes: 20 Servings

INGREDIENTS
- 10 lbs. corn kernels
- 1 tsp salt

DIRECTIONS
1. Prepare the jars as stated in previous pressure canning recipes.
2. Pack the corn into the jars. Do not pack tightly.
3. Cover the corn with clean, boiling water, leaving 1 inch of headspace in each jar.
4. Add salt to each jar.
5. Wipe the rims of each jar with a clean, damp cloth to remove any food residue.
6. Proceed as usual with previous pressure canning recipes, leaving the jars in the canner for 85 minutes.

Pinto Beans

The pressure canning method will be used to process these beans.

Prep: 12 Hours 30 Minutes | Canning Time: 1 Hour 30 Minutes | Makes: 12 Servings

INGREDIENTS
- 9 lbs. pinto beans (or other dried beans)

- 1 tbsp distilled vinegar
- 2 tbsp salt

DIRECTIONS

1. Clean the pinto beans by removing any bad beans, debris, and other undesirables before placing them in a large pot and covering them with water. Add the vinegar and allow the beans to soak overnight or for at least 12 hours. Drain. Alternatively, if you do not have the time to soak the beans for that amount of time, you can place the cleaned beans in a pan of boiling water and boil for 2 minutes. Remove the beans from the heat and allow them to soak for 1 hour then drain.
2. Prepare 6 jars (quarts) as stated in previous pressure canning recipes.
3. Rinse the soaked beans.
4. Place the beans back in the pot and cover with fresh water. Bring this mixture to a boil and boil for 30 minutes.
5. Divide the beans between the jars and fill them with the beans.
6. Put the cooking water over the beans, leaving 1 inch headspace in each jar.
7. Add salt to each jar.
8. Wipe the rims of each jar with a clean, damp cloth to remove any food residue.
9. Proceed as usual with previous pressure canning recipes, leaving the jars in the canner for 90 minutes.

Peppers

This recipe makes use of pressure canning.
Prep: 15 Minutes | Canning Time: 35 Minutes | Makes: 10 Servings

INGREDIENTS

- 10 lbs. peppers
- 1 tsp salt

DIRECTIONS

1. Prepare 6 jars (pints) as stated in previous pressure canning recipes.
2. Peppers can be used whole, quartered, or halved. Remove the core and seeds for each pepper by cutting off the top and pulling out the centers. Use gloves when dealing with hot peppers.
3. Place the peppers on a hot grill, skin side up, and roast until the skin blackens.
4. Remove the peppers from the heat and seal them in a plastic bag. Allow to cool.
5. Remove the peppers from the bag and peel the skin away gently.
6. Equally divide the salt and put it into the jars.

7. Fill the jars with peppers. Do not pack the peppers tightly.
8. Cover the peppers with clean, boiling water, leaving 1 inch of headspace in each jar.
9. Wipe the rims of each jar with a clean, damp cloth to remove any food residue.
10. Proceed as usual with previous pressure canning recipes, leaving the jars in the canner for 35 minutes.

Raw Pack Carrots

Canned carrots can be used in a variety of ways, such as in soups and stews. They can even serve as a snack by sprinkling some cinnamon on them. The following canned carrots recipe relies on a pressure canner. While the following recipe is for raw pack carrots, you can also imitate the recipe with a hot pack version by gently simmering the carrots for 5 minutes before placing them in the jars.

Prep: 15 Minutes | Canning Time: 30 Minutes | Makes: 24 Servings

INGREDIENTS
- 12 lbs. carrots
- 1.5 tsp salt

DIRECTIONS
1. Prepare 6 jars (quarts) as stated in previous pressure canning recipes.
2. Remove the tops of the washed carrots and peel them. Cut the carrots into desired sizes. However, be mindful of not cutting or slicing the carrots too small, as they will turn mushy during the canning process.
3. Equally divide the salt and put it into the jars.
4. Fill the jars with carrot pieces. Do not pack the carrots tightly.
5. Cover the carrots with clean, boiling water, leaving 1 inch of headspace in each jar.
6. Wipe the rims of each jar with a clean, damp cloth to remove any food residue.
7. Proceed as usual with previous pressure canning recipes, leaving the jars in the canner for 30 minutes.

Greens

Examples of greens that can be used in this canning recipe include kale, beet tops, spinach, and swiss chard. The recipe is extraordinarily easy to follow and makes use of a pressure canner.

Prep: 25 Minutes | Canning Time: 1 Hour 30 Minutes | Makes: 7 Servings

INGREDIENTS

- 15 lbs. greens
- 2 tsp salt

DIRECTIONS

1. Prepare 5 jars (quarts) as stated in previous pressure canning recipes.
2. Ensure the greens have been thoroughly cleaned. Blanch them until they have wilted (60 to 90 seconds) then dip them into cold water to stop the cooking process. Drain.
3. Pack the greens loosely into the jars.
4. Top with the equally divided salt.
5. Cover the greens with clean, boiling water, leaving 1 inch of headspace in each jar.
6. Wipe the rims of each jar with a clean, damp cloth to remove any food residue.
7. Proceed as usual with previous pressure canning recipes, leaving the jars in the canner for 90 minutes.

Potatoes

Potatoes are that universal staple product that we all know and love, as it can be prepared in a variety of ways quickly. They can be dressed up, and they can be dressed down. They make a great preserved item for not only everyday life but also as emergency food. The following recipe for home-canned potatoes makes use of a pressure canner.

Prep: 20 Minutes | Canning Time: 40 Minutes | Makes: 10 Servings

INGREDIENTS

- 15 lbs. potatoes
- 2 tsp salt

DIRECTIONS

1. Prepare 5 jars (quarts) as stated in previous pressure canning recipes.
2. Small potatoes can be canned as is, but larger potatoes must be peeled and cut into 1-inch to 2-inch thick pieces.
3. Bring a pot of water to boil over medium heat and boil potatoes for up to 10 minutes, or until they are just fork tender. Drain.
4. Equally divide the salt and put it into the jars.
5. Fill the jars with potato pieces. Do not pack the peppers tightly.
6. Cover the potatoes with clean, boiling water, leaving 1 inch of headspace in each jar.
7. Wipe the rims of each jar with a clean, damp cloth to remove any food residue.

8. Proceed as usual with previous pressure canning recipes, leaving the jars in the canner for 40 minutes.

Pumpkin

Muffins, pies, soups, stews ... all of these and more are recipe options that you can follow when you have canned pumpkin on hand. This recipe shows you how to make your own, using the pressure canner. You can apply the same methodology to items such as winter squash.

Prep: 35 Minutes | Canning Time: 1 Hour 30 Minutes | Makes: 5 Servings

INGREDIENTS
- 15 lbs. pumpkin, peeled and cubed into 1 inch pieces
- 2 tsp salt

DIRECTIONS
1. Prepare 5 jars (quarts) as stated in previous pressure canning recipes.
2. Bring a pot of water to boil over medium heat and boil pumpkin pieces for 2 minutes or until they are just fork tender. Drain.
3. Equally divide the salt and put it into the jars.
4. Fill the jars with pumpkin pieces. Do not pack the pumpkin tightly.
5. Cover the pumpkin pieces with the cooking water, leaving 1 inch of headspace in each jar.
6. Wipe the rims of each jar with a clean, damp cloth to remove any food residue.
7. Proceed as usual with previous pressure canning recipes, leaving the jars in the canner for 40 minutes.

Asparagus

Asparagus is that staple side dish that goes with just about anything. Have it available to prepare your dishes, even during an emergency, by canning with a pressure canner. This particular recipe is for raw pack asparagus, but you can also try the hot pack version by first boiling the asparagus for 3 minutes, and then packing them into the jars.

Prep: 15 Minutes | Canning Time: 40 Minutes | Makes: 10 Servings

INGREDIENTS
- 10 lbs. asparagus
- 1 tsp salt

DIRECTIONS

1. Prepare 5 jars (quarts) as stated in previous pressure canning recipes.
2. Trim the asparagus to fit into the jars.
3. Equally divide the salt and put it into the jars.
4. Loosely pack the asparagus into the jars.
5. Cover the asparagus with clean, boiling water, leaving 1 inch of headspace in each jar.
6. Wipe the rims of each jar with a clean, damp cloth to remove any food residue.
7. Proceed as usual with previous pressure canning recipes, leaving the jars in the canner for 40 minutes.

Canned Soups

There are a variety of soups that you can indulge in, and I have outlined the recipe for canning 2 types below: beef garden soup and vegetable soup. Both of these recipes rely on the pressure canning methodology.

Beef Garden Soup

Prep: 2 Hours 30 Minutes | Canning Time: 1 Hour 15 Minutes | Makes: 13 Servings

INGREDIENTS

- 3 lbs. beef chunks, fat trimmed and cut into 1 inch cubes
- 10 cups beef broth
- 1 potato, chopped
- 1 cup corn
- 2 yellow onions, chopped
- 3 tomatoes, chopped
- 4 carrots, chopped
- 10 garlic cloves, minced
- Salt and pepper to taste
- 1 tbsp olive oil

DIRECTIONS

1. Heat the oil in a pot over medium heat.
2. Add the beef and sauté until the beef has browned.
3. Add the beef broth and bring to a boil. Lower the heat and simmer for 1 hour or until the beef is fork tender.
4. Prepare 13 jars (quarts) as stated in previous pressure canning recipes.

5. Add the remaining ingredients to the pot and bring to a boil. Cover the pot and cook for 10 minutes.
6. Ladle the soup into the prepared jars, leaving 1 inch of headspace in each jar.
7. Wipe the rims of each jar with a clean, damp cloth to remove any food residue.
8. Proceed as usual with previous pressure canning recipes, leaving the jars in the canner for 75 minutes.

Vegetable Soup

Prep: 40 Minutes | Canning Time: 1 Hour | Makes: 12 Servings

INGREDIENTS
- 10 cups vegetable broth
- 4 carrots, chopped
- 1 cup green beans, snapped
- 2 potatoes, chopped
- 2 cups corn
- 2 celery stalks, sliced
- 2 tomatoes, chopped
- 1 cup chopped onion
- 10 garlic cloves, minced
- 1 tsp dried rosemary
- 1 tsp dried thyme
- 1 tsp dried oregano
- 1 tsp dried parsley
- Salt and pepper to taste

DIRECTIONS
1. Prepare 12 jars (quarts) as stated in previous pressure canning recipes.
2. Combine all the ingredients in a pot over medium heat and bring to a boil. Lower the heat and simmer for 10 minutes or until the veggies are just tender.
3. Ladle the soup into the prepared jars, leaving 1 inch of headspace in each jar.
4. Wipe the rims of each jar with a clean, damp cloth to remove any food residue.
5. Proceed as usual with previous pressure canning recipes, leaving the jars in the canner for 60 minutes.

Raw Pack Canned Poultry (Chicken)

Chicken, turkey, quail ... all of this and more fall into the category of poultry. The following recipe can serve as your go-to for raw canning any of them. For the sake of this recipe, chicken will be used as an example. This is a pressure canning recipe.

Prep: 25 Minutes | Canning Time: 1 Hour 30 Minutes | Makes: 5 Servings

INGREDIENTS

- 6 chicken breasts, cubed into 1 inch pieces
- Salt and pepper to taste
- ½ tsp dried rosemary
- ½ tsp dried thyme
- ½ tsp dried oregano

DIRECTIONS

1. Prepare 5 jars (quarts) as stated in previous pressure canning recipes.
2. Season the chicken with the remaining ingredients.
3. Fill each jar with the chicken pieces, leaving 1 ¼ inch headspace in each jar. Gently press the chicken into the jar to maintain this headspace.
4. Add hot water into each jar to fill in any space, leaving 1 inch headspace.
5. Wipe the rims of each jar with a clean, damp cloth to remove any food residue.
6. Proceed as usual with previous pressure canning recipes, leaving the jars in the canner for 90 minutes.

Canned Fish

Whether you make the catch yourself or you purchase your seafood at a store, you can preserve it with canning with a variety of methods. Seafood and fish need to be pressure canned to ensure microorganisms are killed.

This recipe is specific to preserving fatty fish, like salmon and trout. It is a raw packing methodology, but you can also pressure can smoked fish. The canning time and pressure used will be less. It is best to preserve the fish as soon after it was caught or bought to ensure the highest quality.

Prep: 50 Minutes | Canning Time: 1 Hour 50 Minutes | Makes: 10 Servings

INGREDIENTS

- 20 lbs. fish, cleaned, washed, and cut into 1 inch cubes
- 1 ½ cups olive oil

DIRECTIONS

1. Prepare 10 jars (pints) as stated in previous pressure canning recipes.
2. Pack the fish pieces tightly into the jars, leaving 1 ¼ inch of headspace in each jar.
3. Pour the olive oil into each jar, leaving 1 inch headspace.
4. Wipe the rims of each jar with a clean, damp cloth to remove any food residue. Ensure that this cloth was dipped into vinegar beforehand to remove the fatty residue from the rim.
5. Proceed as usual with previous pressure canning recipes, leaving the jars in the canner for 110 minutes.

Canned Rice

The best method of canning rice depends on the type of rice being canned. The 2 following home canning recipes explore how to can white and brown rice.

Water Bath Canning Version - Veggie Brown Rice

This is best for canning brown rice, as it is a low acidity food.

Prep: 1 Hour 30 Minutes | Canning Time: 35 minutes | Makes: 10 Servings

INGREDIENTS

- 20 cups of cooked brown rice, cooled
- 3 yellow onions, diced
- 10 garlic cloves, minced
- 1 tsp dried celery flakes
- 2 tbsp Italian seasoning
- ½ tsp cayenne pepper
- Salt and pepper to taste

DIRECTIONS

1. Prepare 10 jars (pints) and a water bath for water bath canning.
2. Combine all the ingredients well.
3. Loosely fill each jar with the rice mixture, leaving 1 inch headspace.
4. Add hot water into each jar to fill in any space, maintaining the 1 inch headspace.
5. Wipe the rims of each jar with a clean, damp cloth to remove any food residue.

6. Proceed as usual with previous water bath canning recipes, leaving the jars in the canner for 35 minutes.

Water Bath Canning Version – Spanish Rice

This is best for canning white rice, as it is a high acidity food.

Prep: 1 Hour 30 Minutes | Canning Time: 35 minutes | Makes: 10 Servings

INGREDIENTS

- 20 cups of cooked brown rice, cooled
- 1 red bell pepper, chopped
- 1 green bell pepper, chopped
- 3 yellow onions, diced
- 10 garlic cloves, minced
- ¼ cup tomato paste
- 5 tbsp soybean oil
- 1 tbsp vinegar
- Salt and pepper to taste

DIRECTIONS

1. Prepare 10 jars (pints) and a water bath for water bath canning.
2. Combine all the ingredients well.
3. Loosely fill each jar with the rice mixture, leaving 1 inch headspace.
4. Add hot water into each jar to fill in any space, maintaining the 1 inch headspace.
5. Wipe the rims of each jar with a clean, damp cloth to remove any food residue.
6. Proceed as usual with previous water bath canning recipes, leaving the jars in the canner for 35 minutes.

Now that you have information on the food side of prepping, the next book in this series will give you a few recipes for breakfast, lunch, dinner, snacks, and dessert that you can use in dire times.

Book 7:

The Preparation: The Prepper's Recipe List

Not even the end of the world is a good reason to deprive your taste buds of good food. A stereotypical view has been adopted about preppers, one where they have isolated themselves and eat food that would never be consumed under normal circumstances. I am talking about the really nasty stuff.

But we are seeing that there is no stereotypical prepper with a particular look. Disaster after disaster has hit us globally over the last few decades. The Haiti earthquake in 2010. The 9.0 earthquake that triggered a tsunami and nuclear plant melt down in Japan in 2011. Global wildfires that devastated hundreds of thousands of acres of land in the Amazon and Indonesia in 2019. Hurricane Sandy in 2012. Covid-19 in 2020. These disasters, and more, show us that the worst can strike at any time, and the best we can do to be as comfortable and as safe as possible is to prepare as much beforehand. There is no one face to preparation. There is just a mindset.

What you will eat if you are cut off from other people and the typical modern conveniences, like supermarkets and restaurants, must be figured out. You do not have to be a top-of-the-line chef to ensure your tummy and taste buds remain happy no matter what. This section of the book arms you with a few easy-to-create recipes no matter the time of day.

The Cookbook Introduction

Of course, you must stock food that is ready to eat without any preparation whatsoever in case of a catastrophe. Crackers and canned foods are examples of this. But nothing beats a hot meal, even if you have to make use of the great outdoors to make that hot meal. Ways to cook outdoors include:

Outdoor Grill

Many newer grill models make use of gas tanks or electricity as a fuel source. However, you can also use charcoal. All you have to do is ensure that your fuel source is also handy.

Swedish Fire Log Candle

This tool for cooking is more rustic than the last. The Swedish fire log candle is created with a large log planted upright. At least 4 vertical cuts are created along the length of the log running down the entire length. A fire is lit in the center of this creation to cook food.

Rocket Stove

You can create a rocket stove fast and easily, even under the most trying times while outdoors. All you need are a few handy items, such as used cans and a pail, and you will be cooking in no time at all.

Hobo Stove

This is an even easier-to-create version of a rocket stove. All you need is a can and the know-how, and you are set to cook.

Dutch Oven

This is a classic tool for cooking, as it keeps the heat well. As a result, there is a long list of meals, like soups, stews, and even desserts, like pies, that can be cooked using a Dutch oven.

Wood Burning Stove

This tool can not only serve as a way to cook food but also as a heat source.

Part of ensuring that you are prepared food-wise for any emergency is ensuring that you have the tools for food preparation. I would stock at least two of these tools, if I were you. Now that you understand the intricacies of food preparation, even under the most trying times, let's get down to actually doing it with tasty recipes for any time of day.

Chapter 1 – The Prepper's Breakfast

Cornmeal Mush

This is a hearty, filling meal to start your day off right.

Prep: 5 Minutes | Cooking Time: 40 Minutes | Makes: 2 Servings

INGREDIENTS
- 1 cup cornmeal
- 4 cups water
- 1 tsp salt
- ¼ cup dried cherries

DIRECTIONS
1. Bring the water to a boil.
2. Stir in the salt and ensure dissolved. Alternatively, you can use ½ tbsp of sugar instead if you prefer something sweet.
3. Stir in the cornmeal slowly and continuously to ensure lumps do not form.
4. Allow the cornmeal to boil for about half an hour.
5. Stir in the dried cherries.
6. Serve warm.

Corn Dodgers

These are a form of cornbread that can be eaten alone or with chili or stew.

Prep: 15 Minutes | Cooking Time: 25 Minutes | Makes: 4 Servings

INGREDIENTS
- 4 cups cornmeal
- 4 cups milk
- 2 tsp baking powder
- 4 tbsp butter
- 1 tbsp sugar

- 1 tsp salt

DIRECTIONS

1. Combine all the ingredients, except the baking powder, in a pot and place over medium heat. Stir occasionally and cook for about 10 minutes or until the mixture thickens.
2. Remove the cornmeal mixture from the heat and allow it to sit for 5 minutes.
3. Stir in the baking powder.
4. Preheat a griddle or Dutch oven.
5. Pour small scoops of the mixture onto the preheated surface. Cook for 10 minutes or until the edges of the corn dodgers have browned. Flip halfway through.
6. Serve warm.

Cured Bacon

This recipe is a throwback to when pioneers used to cure meat to preserve the pieces. It does not hurt that the results are so tasty.

Prep: 4 Weeks | Makes: 20 Servings

INGREDIENTS

- 10 lbs. picnic arm roast with skin on
- 2 cups brown sugar
- 2 cups salt
- 3 tbsp saltpeter
- 1 cup molasses

DIRECTIONS

1. Combine the sugar, saltpeter, and molasses in a bowl to create a brine.
2. Sprinkle the ham with salt.
3. Pour the brine over the ham.
4. Place the ham in a barrel to cure for at least 4 weeks.
5. Cut the ham into thin strips to serve.

Hasty Bread

This recipe allows you to get your bread fix, no matter what.

Prep: 1 Hour 15 Minutes | Cooking Time: 1 Hour | Makes: 4 Servings

INGREDIENTS

- 4 cups flour
- 2 tsp salt
- 3 tbsp yeast
- 1 ½ cup warm water

DIRECTIONS

1. Sift the flour into a bowl. Stir in the salt and yeast.
2. Add the water and knead for 5 minutes or until the dough is elastic.
3. Cover the dough with a kitchen towel and allow it to rest for 10 minutes.
4. Knead the dough for another 5 minutes.
5. Allow to rest for another 30 minutes.
6. Create the desired shape of bread.
7. Bake for 1 hour or until the bread is golden brown.
8. Serve as desired.

Chapter 2 – The Prepper's Lunch

2-Ingredient Beef Stew

Warm your body and spirit with this comforting and whole recipe, which makes use of beef stew and diced tomatoes that you canned at home or bought at the store.

Prep: 5 Minutes | Cooking Time: 5 Minutes | Makes: 2 Servings

INGREDIENTS
- 1 can beef stew
- 1 cup tomatoes, diced

DIRECTIONS
1. Combine the ingredients in a pan and place them over medium heat.
2. Bring to a boil.
3. Serve warm.

Prepper's Pizza

This common delight does not have to be absent from your diet, even during disastrous times.

Prep: 1 Hour 15 Minutes | Cooking Time: 30 Minutes | Makes: 3 Servings

INGREDIENTS
- 2 cups white flour
- 2 tbsp yeast
- 1 tsp salt
- 1 tbsp sugar
- ¾ cup warm water
- 2 tbsp olive oil

DIRECTIONS
1. Sift the flour into a bowl. Stir in the salt, sugar, and yeast.
2. Add the water and knead for 5 minutes or until the dough is elastic.

3. Pour the oil over the dough. Cover with a kitchen towel and allow to rest for 1 hour.
4. Knead the dough for 5 more minutes.
5. Roll the dough out into a pizza pan.
6. Allow to rest for 10 minutes.
7. Top with desired toppings.
8. Bake for 30 minutes in an oven, preheated to 325 degrees F, or until the edges have browned.
9. Slice and serve warm.

Chicken and Dumplings

This is the ultimate comfort food, and you never have to do without it.

Prep: 20 Minutes | Cooking Time: 45 Minutes | Makes: 6 Servings

INGREDIENTS
- 1 can chicken
- 1 tbsp Italian seasoning
- Salt and pepper to taste
- 1 tbsp cornstarch
- 1 can corn
- 1 cup flour
- 2 tbsp butter
- 3 cups chicken broth

DIRECTIONS
1. Combine the chicken, seasoning, salt, pepper, cornstarch and corn in a pot over medium heat. Bring to a boil. Lower the heat and simmer for 5 minutes.
2. Combine the remaining ingredients in a bowl to create a soft dough.
3. Use your fingers to pick small pieces of the dough. Drop them into the chicken mixture. Stir and simmer for 30 minutes or until the sauce has thickened.
4. Serve warm.

Lemony Chicken Pasta

This dish is quick and easy to make, yet you would never tell based on how tasty it is.

Prep: 15 Minutes | Cooking Time: 20 Minutes | Makes: 4 Servings

INGREDIENTS
- 1 can chicken, drained
- 3 cups cooked pasta
- 3 tbsp oil
- ½ tbsp vinegar
- 2 tbsp lemon juice
- 1 cup chicken broth
- 1 cup canned spinach
- 3 garlic cloves, minced
- 1 tbsp dried parsley
- Salt and pepper to taste

DIRECTIONS
1. Combine the pasta, vinegar, and ⅓ of the oil in a bowl.
2. Heat the remaining oil in a skillet over medium heat and sauté the chicken until all sides have been browned.
3. Add the chicken to the pasta. Combine well.
4. Sauté the garlic in the juice remaining in the pan for 2 minutes or until fragrant.
5. Stir in the lemon juice.
6. Stir in the chicken broth and spinach. Bring to a boil. Lower the heat and simmer for 10 minutes or until the sauce has thickened.
7. Season with salt and pepper.
8. Stir in the parsley.
9. To serve, spoon the sauce over the pasta.

Jerky Gravy

This gravy can be used to elevate many dishes, like potatoes and biscuits.

Prep: 10 Minutes | Cooking Time: 15 Minutes | Makes: 4 Servings

INGREDIENTS

- 2 cups jerky, chopped
- 2 tbsp butter
- 3 tbsp flour
- 1 cup milk
- Salt and pepper to taste

DIRECTIONS

1. Heat the butter in a pan over medium heat. Add the jerky and cook until the jerky has become crispy. Remove the jerky from the pan and place it in a bowl.
2. Combine the flour and milk in a bowl to create a thickener. Pour into the grease left in the pan. Stir and cook until a smooth sauce has formed.
3. Return the jerky to the pan. Stir to combine well.
4. Serve warm as desired.

Chapter 3 – The Prepper's Dinner

5-Ingredient Mac & Cheese

The following recipe can serve as the base to add more ingredients. Therefore, you can create variations by adding canned or dried items, like fish and chicken to the dish.

Prep: 10 Minutes | Cooking Time: 10 Minutes | Makes: 2 Servings

INGREDIENTS

- 4 cups cooked elbow macaroni
- ½ cup dried cheese powder
- 3 tbsp powdered buttermilk
- ¾ cup water
- Salt and pepper to taste

DIRECTIONS

1. Combine the dried cheese powder, powdered buttermilk, and water to create a cheese paste.
2. Combine the cheese paste and cooked macaroni.
3. Season with salt and pepper.
4. Add any desired additional ingredients or serve as is.

Pasta and Red Sauce

This recipe is plain and simple with no frills, but it is also oh so good!

Prep: 5 Minutes | Cooking Time: 35 Minutes | Makes: 2 Servings

INGREDIENTS

- 4 cups cooked pasta
- 1 can diced tomatoes
- 3 tbsp Italian seasoning
- Salt and pepper to taste

DIRECTIONS

1. Combine the tomatoes, Italian seasoning, salt, and pepper in a pot over medium heat. Bring to a boil. Lower the heat and simmer for 25 minutes.
2. To serve, ladle the sauce over the cooked pasta. Serve warm.

Cream of Mushroom Soup

While this recipe is focused on using mushrooms as the main ingredient, you can substitute this with other items like chicken or potatoes. It is a versatile recipe.

Prep: 10 Minutes | Cooking Time: 25 Minutes | Makes: 5 Servings

INGREDIENTS
- 1 cup dried potato flakes
- 4 tbsp dried low sodium vegetable broth
- 1 tbsp powdered milk
- 4 cups water
- 4 cups dried sliced mushrooms
- 1 cup canned mixed vegetables
- Salt and pepper to taste

DIRECTIONS
1. Combine the dried mushrooms and water in a pot over medium heat. Bring to a boil. Lower the heat and simmer for 10 minutes.
2. Add the potato flakes, dried veggie broth, and powdered milk and cook until the sauce has thickened.
3. Stir in the mixed vegetables. Cook for 2 minutes.
4. Season with salt and pepper.
5. Serve warm.

Corned Beef

Corned beef can be added to rice, pasta, soup, stews, and so many more dishes.

Prep: 10 Days | Makes: 24 Servings

INGREDIENTS

- 8 lbs. of beef
- 2 cups salt
- 2 cups molasses
- 2 tbsp saltpeter
- 1 tbsp pepper

DIRECTIONS

1. Combine all the ingredients, except the beef, in a bowl.
2. Rub the beef with the salt mixture.
3. Let the beef sit for at least 10 days, turning daily.
4. Mince the beef when serving.

Potato Cakes

This recipe is the combination of two great things: potatoes and pancakes.

Prep: 15 Minutes | Cooking Time: 5 Minutes | Makes: 4 Servings

INGREDIENTS

- 5 potatoes, peeled and grated
- 1 ½ tbsp salt
- ½ cup milk
- 2 eggs
- 1 cup flour

DIRECTIONS

1. Combine all the ingredients in a bowl.
2. Heat a greased pan.
3. Add spoonsful of the potato cake batter into the heated pan and cook for 5 minutes or until golden brown on both sides. Flip halfway through.
4. Serve warm with syrup or desired toppings.

Chapter 4 – The Prepper's Snacks

Hardtack

This item goes by many other names, including hard bread, tooth duller, and ship's biscuits. It has been eaten as a survivalist food for centuries and uses basic ingredients that any good prepper will have on hand.

Hardtack can be quite bland on its own, so beef up the taste by soaking it in liquids, like coffee or soup. Doing so also softens them up for an easier eating experience. They can be topped with honey, jellies, fruit preserves, and jams.

Prep: 20 Minutes | Cooking Time: 1 Hour | Makes: 5 Servings

INGREDIENTS
- 5 cups flour
- 1 cup water

DIRECTIONS
1. Add the water to a bowl.
2. Slowly add the flour. Mix until a hard dough forms. You will not be able to stir this.
3. Knead the dough into a ball.
4. Lightly flour a working surface and roll out the dough with a rolling pin to create ½ inch thick rectangle.
5. Cut the dough into squares about 2-inch-by-2-inch.
6. Transfer the squares to an ungreased cookie sheet.
7. Poke holes into the squares with a fork.
8. Bake in an oven, preheated to 375 degrees F, for 1 hour. Flip halfway through.
9. Allow to cool and serve.

Traditional Pemmican

We were gifted with this dish by Native Americans. The name comes from the Cree word for fat, as pemmican is made from combining meat with fat.

Prep: 15 Minutes | Cooking Time: 15 Minutes | Makes: 8 Servings

INGREDIENTS

- 2 lbs. bacon
- 1 lb. beef fat
- ¼ lb. jerky
- 1 cup dried cranberries
- 1 cup cashews
- ⅓ cup honey
- 1 tsp salt

DIRECTIONS

1. Cook the bacon and beef fat over medium heat to render the fat. Remove the bacon once it is crisp and place it on paper towels to soak up the grease.
2. Fry the jerky in the rendered fat until crisp. Remove the jerky and add it to the same plate as the crisp bacon. Set aside the rendered fat.
3. Add bacon and jerky to a food processor and process until a coarse mixture is developed.
4. Add the processed meat to a bowl. Combine with the salt, cranberries, and cashews.
5. Add the rendered fat and honey into the mixture and combine well.
6. Pour the mixture onto a cooking sheet. Spread into an even layer.
7. Freeze the mixture overnight.
8. Slice into 2-inch-by-3-inch sized bars.
9. Wrap the individual pieces in wax paper and place them in a resealable plastic container.
10. Freeze until ready to eat.
11. Thaw, heat, and serve when desired.

Jerky

This is an item that you can keep in your food prep kit for months and months. It is especially perfect when you have spare meat in your freezer.

Prep: 12 Hours | Cooking Time: 6 Hours 15 Minutes| Makes: 20 Servings

INGREDIENTS

- 4 lbs. venison, fat trimmed and sliced into ¼ inch thick slices
- 1 cup soy sauce
- ⅓ cup Worchester sauce
- 1 tsp curing salt

- 2 tsp garlic powder
- 1 tbsp onion powder
- Salt and pepper to taste

DIRECTIONS

1. Combine all the ingredients, except the venison, in a bowl to create a marinade.
2. Add the venison pieces. Mix well. Cover the bowl and refrigerate it overnight.
3. Preheat a smoker to 160 degrees F.
4. Remove the marinated venison from the refrigerator and drain.
5. Lay out the venison strips on the racks of your smoker. Smoke for 6 hours, checking every 2 to 3 hours.
6. Finish the jerky by baking in an oven, preheated at 200 degrees F, for 15 minutes or until it just begins to splinter.
7. Store the cooled jerky in a glass jar or a vacuum-sealed storage bag.

Bannock

This is a tried and true survival food, as it has been around for a long time. It uses a few ingredients to create and has a long shelf life, in addition to being a highly nutritious food. Just like hardtack, this snack can be eaten alone, but the taste can be elevated when it is accompanied by liquids, such as coffee or other items, like jellies and preserves.

Prep: 15 Minutes | Cooking Time: 20 Minutes | Makes: 15 Servings

INGREDIENTS

- 5 cups flour
- ½ tsp salt
- 2 tsp baking powder
- 1 tbsp sugar
- 1 cup raisins, chopped
- 1 tsp dried rosemary, chopped
- 1 ½ cups buttermilk

DIRECTIONS

1. Combine the flour, salt, baking powder, and sugar in a bowl.
2. Create a well in the center of the flour mixture and pour in the buttermilk. Mix to create a sticky dough.

3. Incorporate the raisins and rosemary into the mixture.
4. Place the dough on a cookie sheet and gently flatten it into a 1 inch thick layer.
5. Bake in an oven preheated at 300 degrees F for 20 minutes or until the top has browned.
6. Allow to cool.
7. Slice and serve.

Dried Fruit

Dried fruit develops a natural resistance to spoilage and are easy to store. They take up less space since they weigh less than fresh food, even though they have the same nutritional value. Keeping dried fruit as part of your food preparation kit allows you to gain a snack that is low in fat and sodium but high in the important nutritional values of fiber, minerals, and vitamins that you need to stay healthy. Whilst certain ingredients are used in the recipe below, you can customize the items used to suit your taste.

Prep: 20 Minutes | Cooking Time: 10 Hours | Makes: 8 Servings

INGREDIENTS
- 1 cup ripe banana, sliced
- 1 apple, cored and sliced
- 1 pear, cored and sliced
- 1 cup strawberries, sliced
- ½ cup lemon juice
- ½ cup water

DIRECTIONS
1. Combine the water and lemon juice.
2. Dip the fruit slices into the lemon water mixture to help preserve the natural color of the fruits.
3. Cover oven racks with cheesecloth and place the fruit slices on them.
4. Place the racks into the oven, which should be preheated to 145 degrees F. Leave the oven door slightly open and bake the fruit for between 5 and 10 hours or until the fruit has completely dried. The fruit will have a leathery consistency when done.
5. Allow to cool and transfer to an airtight bag. Store in a cool, dry area.

Ration Bars

You don't have to be in the military to enjoy ration bars. You can create your own at home with the following recipe. These bars are energy-rich, as they are packed full of protein and fat.

Prep: 15 Minutes | Makes: 15 Servings

INGREDIENTS
- 5 cups oats
- ¼ cup chia seeds
- ¼ cup almond flour
- 5 scoops protein powder
- 1 cup of honey
- 1 cup of coconut oil
- ⅓ cup almond butter

DIRECTIONS
1. Combine the oats, chia seeds, almond flour, and protein powder in a bowl.
2. Combine the remaining ingredients in a microwavable bowl and microwave in 25-second bursts until consistent liquid is achieved.
3. Add the honey mixture to the dry ingredients and mix well to develop a hard but crumbly texture.
4. Transfer the mixture onto a cookie sheet lined with parchment paper and gently press into a 1 inch thick layer.
5. Freeze for 12 hours.
6. Slice and store the individual bars in airtight storage bags.

Chapter 5 – The Prepper's Dessert

This dessert can soothe any sweet tooth. In addition to being a dessert, it can also be eaten as breakfast or dinner.

Prep: 10 Minutes | Cooking Time: 10 Minutes | Makes: 2 Servings

INGREDIENTS

- 3 cups cooked white rice
- 1 tsp salt
- 1 tbsp sugar
- ½ cup raisins
- 1 tsp ground nutmeg
- 1 tsp vanilla extract
- 1 cup milk
- 2 eggs, beaten

DIRECTIONS

1. Heat the rice and milk over medium heat.
2. Add in the remaining ingredients and cook until the eggs are well done.
3. Serve warm.

Chocolate Syrup

This is a wonderful topping for your traditional snack and breakfast items, like ice cream and pancakes, but it can also be used to enhance the flavor of some of the recipes outlined above, such as hardtack and bannock.

Prep: 2 Minutes | Cooking Time: 5 Minutes | Makes: 20 Servings

INGREDIENTS

- ⅓ cup cocoa powder
- 1 cup sugar
- 1 cup water
- 1 tsp vanilla extract
- A pinch of salt

DIRECTIONS

1. Combine all the ingredients, except the water and vanilla extract, in a saucepan.
2. Stir in the water to create a smooth mixture. Place this over medium heat. Bring to a boil. Allow to boil for 1 minute.
3. Remove the mixture from the heat and allow to cool.
4. Stir in the vanilla extract.
5. Serve as desired.

Raspberry Crumble Bars

In addition to being a great dessert, you can serve these bars as a breakfast item, as they are full of protein.

Prep: 15 Minutes | Cooking Time: 40 Minutes | Makes: 18 Servings

INGREDIENTS

- 3 cups oats
- 3 cups flour, plus 2 tbsp
- 1 ½ cup brown sugar
- 1 cup melted butter
- 1 tsp baking powder
- 1 cup frozen raspberries
- 1 tbsp lemon juice
- ¼ cup granulated sugar
- 1 tbsp cornstarch
- ½ tsp salt

DIRECTIONS

1. Place the raspberries in a colander and run warm water over them. Allow to sit for an hour so that they soften.
2. Combine the raspberries with the granulated sugar, 2 tbsp of flour, cornstarch, and lemon juice in a bowl.
3. Mix the remaining ingredients in a bowl to create a crumble mixture.
4. Layer half of the crumbled mixture into the bottom of a 9 x 13 baking pan lined with parchment paper. Bake in an oven that has been preheated to 350 degrees F for 10 minutes.

5. Remove the crumble mixture from the oven and arrange the raspberry mixture on top. Then top this with the remaining crumble and bake for another 30 minutes.
6. Allow to cool.
7. Slice and serve.

Rice Pudding

This is comfort food that has been around for a long time and does not look like it will be going anywhere any time soon, especially since it is easy to prepare, even under strenuous circumstances.

Prep: 5 Minutes | Cooking Time: 15 Minutes | Makes: 3 Servings

INGREDIENTS
- 3 cups cooked rice
- 3 cups almond milk
- ¼ cup sugar
- ½ tsp vanilla extract
- ¼ tsp salt
- ¼ tsp ground cinnamon

DIRECTIONS
1. Combine all the ingredients, except the vanilla extract, in a saucepan over medium heat. Bring to a boil.
2. Lower heat and simmer for 10 minutes or until the mixture has thickened.
3. Remove the rice pudding from the heat and stir in the vanilla extract.
4. Allow to cool for about 1 minute so that the mixture thickens further.
5. Serve warm.

Now that you've got the preparation phase of being a prepper down, the next book will get you started with defenses and how you can defend your home during disasters and from intruders.

Book 8:

The Defense: Protecting Your Home

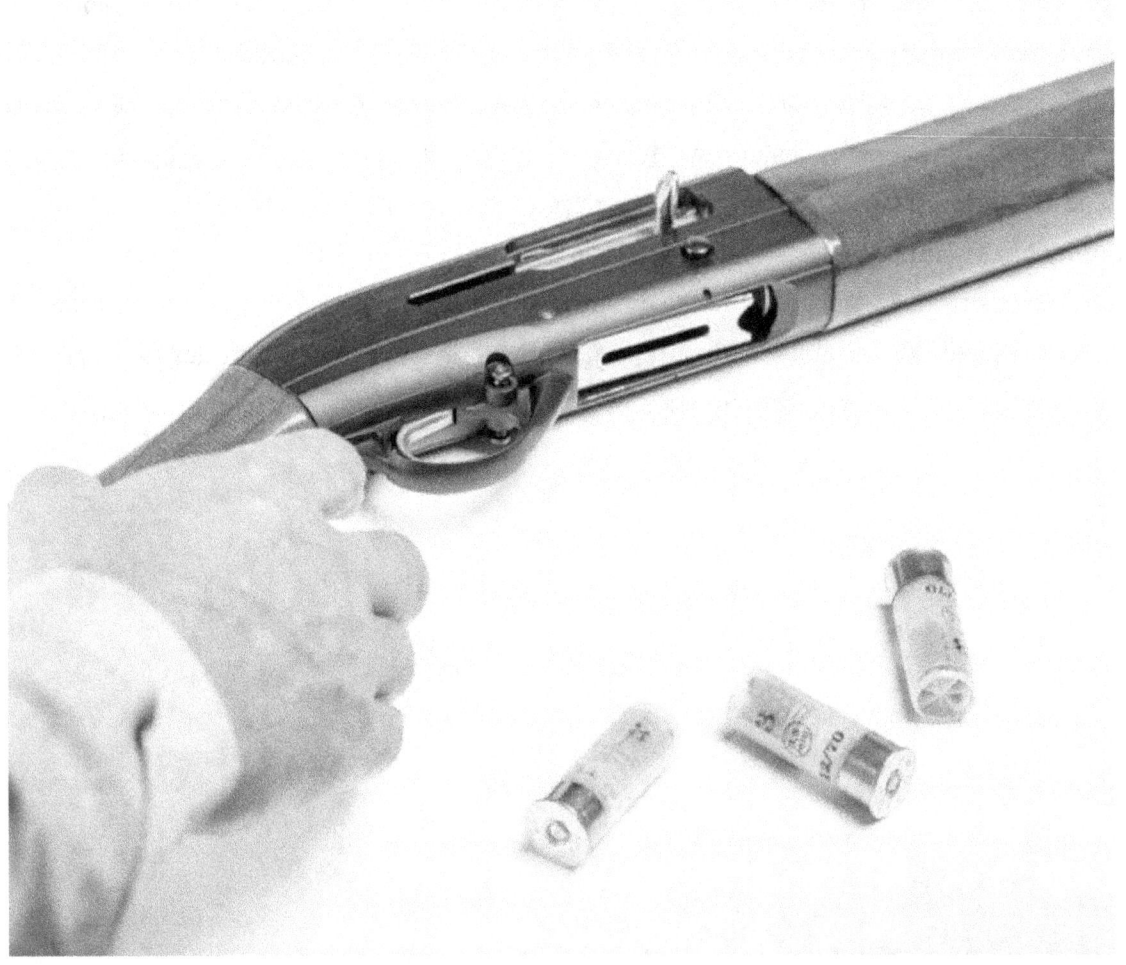

In 2019 alone, American homes and businesses sustained nearly $13 billion worth of damage or loss from burglaries and other types of theft.

Did that fact shock you? If it did, you'd best prepare yourself because the statistics only get worse. On average, a burglary happens every 30 seconds in the United States. This means that there are 2 burglaries every single minute of the day and over 3000 every single day. These numbers were not pulled out of thin air but rather provided by the FBI. Most of these occurrences are because those places lacked security measures, like the installation of alarms and security systems.

I do not provide you with these statistics to scare you. Rather, I give them to you to prompt you into acting to better protect your home.

When we think of disaster, we tend to think of natural phenomena and pandemics. However, there are other threats that we need to protect ourselves, our loved ones, and our property from, and one of the most pressing is theft.

Being burglarized does not just leave you in the hole financially at times, nor is it limited to missing material possessions. There is also a psychological impact. We grow mistrustful and feel violated. Being the victim of burglary can lead to such emotional distress that the victim suffers from depression, anxiety disorders, and posttraumatic stress disorder (PTSD) to name a few of the mental illnesses that can result.

It is unfortunate to state that the probability of being burglarized increases when there are extenuating circumstances, like after natural disasters and during the fallout of pandemics. People become desperate when even the basic items needed to survive are in short supply. Often, they turn to crime as a means of getting these items, so homes are a primary target. While there is no absolute guarantee that you can stop burglars and other nefarious individuals from entering your home unlawfully, you can put measures in place to minimize the risk. This section is dedicated to helping you ensure that your home is not an easy target for burglaries or other criminal acts whether under normal circumstances or more stressful times.

The Defense Introduction

One of the first events that occur in the plot of disaster movies is looting at the first announcement or occurrence of a crisis. Why? Because it is almost certain to happen in real life, too. A good prepper is also prepared to lessen the chances of their home being looted and has measures in place to protect himself from bodily harm if intruders do penetrate their defenses. This preparation is not as simple as arming yourself with firearms. It goes beyond that and includes fortifying your home and the people who live in it. These measures are not just great for protecting people physically, but they will also give you peace of mind and allow you to sleep more soundly, whether or not times are typical or not.

Under normal circumstances, intruders will look for weak points in your home's security system (or lack thereof) to gain entry. They typically work alone or in small groups and act out elaborate plots to make this entry as inconspicuous as possible. As a result, we often hear news reports of people posing as innocent-looking workers, like repairmen, pool cleaners, and gardeners, as they commit these crimes. Most people do not look twice when they see people in such uniforms and roles in their communities and neighborhoods. Therefore, this is the opportunity these criminals take advantage of during the norm of day-to-day life.

Under not-so-normal circumstances, such as the aftermath of a natural disaster, intruders tend to take a different approach. They gain strength in numbers and invade homes in gangs. They are more ruthless than your everyday home invaders and carry weapons. Often, desperation fuels their shenanigans. That spells disaster if they come upon an occupied home.

Ideally, a prepper will have a bunker to retreat to, as well as weapons of their own to defend themselves, but even if that is not the case, it is wise to learn to protect your home in ways that:

1. Deter intruders. This is the first measure of defense, and it involves making your home unattractive or inaccessible to intruders.
2. Delay intruders. This is the second measure of protection against intruders and occurs only if you are unable to deter these people away from your home. The point of this measure is to buy yourself time to get to safety by stalling the intruders' entry for as long as possible.
3. Defend your home. This is the last point of protection. If the intruders are insistent, delays will likely ultimately fail if you cannot get assistance from authorities. In such a case, you need to be able to safeguard yourself and your loved ones from harm.

Let's start developing your home defenses with the first measure of protection: deterring intruders. To do that, you need to get in their head and determine how they might try to enter your home so that you can nullify those points of entry. No matter the circumstances surrounding the act of intrusion, these intruders can only enter a home after finding a weak spot. Let's take a look at possible weak spots and how you can strengthen them.

During Vacation

An empty house that is undefended by its residents is one of the easiest for intruders to target, so they do quite often. There are times when people normally take vacation, so these criminals are often biding their time to target homes. Such times include the months of July and August when many kids are on summer break and Christmastime.

Even outside of such times, you might inadvertently be leaving clues for these criminals, stating that you are away from your home for extended periods. In this day and age, one of the most obvious signs of an empty house is posts on social media. They serve the same as slapping a big, red sign with a welcome mat for intruders.

Other signs that you are on vacation include:
- Having no animals on the property when there are obvious signs of them at other times, such as the barking of dogs.
- A mailbox that is overcrowded with deliveries.
- Newspapers and other similar items are scattered unchecked on the lawn or the front area of the house.
- Having no lights on, on the property for days on end.
- Having no vehicle parked in the driveway when there usually is.
- Having no response to the doorbell for extended periods.

So, how do you deter criminals away from your home when you are away on vacation? There are several ways, and this list includes:
- Do not announce your vacations on social media until after you have returned home. On the other hand, it is a good idea to inform a few trusted neighbors and friends that you are gone so that they keep an eye out for your property.
- Hire a pet sitter so that, not only does your house have animal activity, but they are an extra set of eyes on the property. You can get a security dog to protect your property during those times, as well.
- Ask someone to pick up your mail from your mailbox regularly so that it does not pile up.
- Hire a house sitter so that there is activity, such as the lights turned on while you are away.
- Ask a trusted friend or neighbor to periodically park a vehicle on your property.

The point of all these measures is to confuse and, therefore, deter intruders as they are not sure of your whereabouts.

An Open Garage Door

A garage door becomes a weak point and possible entry into a home due to complacency. Many people feel safe in the neighborhoods, so they forget to lock garage doors whether they are at home or away. Having to force open a garage door is unattractive to thieves, as it can attract attention. Therefore, you can beef up your security with the simple act of locking your garage doors. Enhance your security by adding security cameras that are positioned in clear sight above this area. Many criminals will shy away from your property if they know their activity is being monitored and recorded by such a security measure.

Windows

Again, complacency can be a killer. Always remember to lock your windows, especially when you are away. The type of windows that you install in your home can also be a deterrent to thieves. Simple glass windows can be breached by breaking. On the other hand, it is not so easy to break pre-laminated glass. Even though it is a more expensive option, it is an effective deterrent.

Doors Around Your Home

Just like with your garage and windows, be sure to lock your doors as the first step of security, especially when you are not at home. Ordinary doors will not serve as an effective deterrent, however.

Weakly constructed doors can be breached with a simple, well-placed kick. More clever intruders can use a credit card to slide the locks on your typical door with no lock-picking tools required.

Lessen the chances of intruders getting in through the front door by implementing the next few tips:
- Install a peephole so that you can learn the identity of people before opening your door to them.
- Change your locks if you notice that they are damaged, rusting, or worn out. Do the same thing with your door hinges.
- Get secure locks that outdo the standard. Options include a deadbolt lock, a night latch, or a multi-point locking system. I would recommend using more than one type of lock on your doors.
- Reinforce your door's locking system with items such as deadbolts and door chains.
- Install a security strike plate, which is a piece of metal specifically designed to prevent your door from weakening when being struck.
- Install a door jammer, which reinforces your door security if it is struck in much the same way that a security strike plate does.

The Rear Door

Many people use French doors as back doors, as they provide a view into the outdoors and backyard. Many people also leave them open as a way that other family members and friends can get into the home while they are away. This is also a way for intruders to get in easily. They can be easily broken, even if they are locked. Replace French doors with more secure options, like wooden doors.

Chapter 1 – The Outdoor Defense

Your home's defense is made up of two parts, and those are the outdoor and indoor defenses. Let's discuss how you can beef up security in both areas, starting with the outdoor space, as intruders first need to breach the outdoor security before they can get in. Luckily, there are lots of things that you can do to make it difficult for intruders to target your home. Such measures that are specific to your outdoor space include:

Not Leaving Your Keys Outside

It is understandably quite a headache if you forget your keys, and most of us are tempted to leave a spare somewhere outside of our home in case of such an event. Intruders are on to this mindset; therefore, they look in the typical hiding spaces, such as under a welcome mat, above the doorframe, on a window ledge, or under a fake rock in your flower garden. They are smart enough to copy your keys if found, so they reenter your home at times that are convenient to them. Avoid leaving spare keys around your home so you can avoid such an occurrence.

If you must hide a spare key somewhere in your yard be sure to place it in an inconspicuous place, such as inside of your guard dog kennel, inside of a coded lockbox that is installed out of sight, or inside a PVC pipe that has been capped on both ends and buried in your yard.

Never Put Your Name and Address on Your Keys

You might consider leaving your name, number, and address on your keys in case they ever get lost. However, this is a double-edged sword, as it can also serve to advertise your home location to possible Intruders.

If you ever lose your keys and are not able to retrieve them from a credible source, the safest course of action is to have your locks changed.

Ensuring Your Outdoor Areas are Well Lit

Intruders love the cover of the dark to act out their crimes. That is why so many criminals act in dead of night. Install lights on your property as a deterrent. Ways that you can ensure that around and in your home are well lit include:
- Ensuring that your garage area and door entrances have lights placed above them.
- Installing porch lights with dusk to dawn timers that allow you to conserve electricity.

- Installing motion sensor lights in your yard and around doors. They come on whenever motion is sensed and keep your electricity bill as low as possible. They can trick criminals into thinking there is activity in and around the home when you are away.
- Install exterior and internal lights with a vacation timer so that it appears that someone is home while you are on vacation or away for extended periods.
- Install low-voltage and solar landscape lights around landscaped areas.

Keeping Your Outdoor Spaces Neat

A cluttered yard provides multiple hiding spaces for intruders. Keep your yard and other outdoor spaces as tidy as possible without any large structures where intruders can hide or watch you unobserved.

Keeping your yard clean also has the dual purpose of allowing your neighbors to easily see if there is suspicious activity going on in your space. Multiple eyes checking for your property is better than just your own.

Securing Your Mail

The theft of packages is highly common and a rising occurrence. These people can easily steal things that have been left in your mailbox or on your doorstep. Set up times for delivery while you are at home or ask for these packages to be held at your nearest post office for you to pick up at a time that is convenient for you. This also serves the dual purpose of not giving intruders a reason to target your home for heavier crimes.

You may also consider investing in a PO box to minimize theft and an overflowing mailbox that serves as a telltale sign that you have been away from home for an extended amount of time.

Being Cautious of People Who Come up to Your Door

This precaution does not only serve strangers. It also applies to delivery people, repairmen, and even law enforcement officials. If anyone comes to your door unexpectedly and without invitation, be on high alert. Have defense mechanisms, such as pepper spray, ready and ask for this person to identify themselves and their purpose on your property. If you have any doubt about this person's identity or intentions, do not open the door and call law enforcement.

Enhancing Your Landscape for Security

How you landscape your yard can either invite intruders or keep them away. Examples of landscape features that make your home attractive to intruders include:

- Overgrown hedges in front of your home where they can easily hide.
- Trees that provide access to second and third-story windows.
- Trees and shrubs that cover doors and windows and provide a hiding spot.

Deter trespassers from coming onto your properties by keeping hedges and shrubs trimmed to less than 3 feet tall and ensure that plant life that grows to a significant height is planted away from your doors and windows.

Another way to enhance home security with your landscape choices is to use thorny or prickly shrubs underneath windows. Your options are quite beautiful. Roses, for example, add color and vibrancy to your yard, but their thorns ward off intruders. More options include:

- Common Holly
- Firethorn
- Fuchsia
- Juniper
- Blue Spruce
- Oleaster

Cacti and sunny succulents, like prickly pear cactus, also provide great options in drier and hotter climates. Additionally, you can consider plants that provide a food item in addition to having thorns and prickles. Some of these include:

- Citrus trees, like lemons and limes
- Wild plums
- Goji berries
- Gooseberries
- Raspberries
- Pomegranates

Setting Alarms on Your Driveway

Such alarms are powered by technology that detects motion and emits an alarm of some sort that alerts you to possible intrusion. The exact specifications of the type of alarm that will be set in your driveway depend on your budget and your specific needs.

Setting up this alarm does not just secure your driveway from entry by intruders but also serves as a means of deterring them from parking a vehicle to steal large amounts of physical items or larger items from your home. Not many people would sense anything amiss if they see someone loading a vehicle that is parked in your driveway with items. However, it certainly calls attention if loud noises come from that area.

There are also driveway alarms that allow you to observe your home via video from remote locations. Driveway alarms can also be installed in other areas such as around trees, walls, and fence posts.

Installing Fences

Secure the perimeter of your yard with a sturdy fence. A wooden fence option is not the most secure, but it is better than nothing. More secure options include:
- Heras fencing
- Wooden boarding
- Chain link fencing
- Metal hoarding
- Mesh panel fencing
- Palisade fencing

If you do not have the budget for physical fencing, or it is regulated within your community, you can consider planting thorny shrubs and bushes along the perimeter. Such plants can also be placed just inside fences as another layer of protection.

Adding Locks to Your Gates

All fences will include the installation of gates to get in and out of the yard. Therefore, the security of these gates needs to be ensured. Use premium quality locks to ensure that this security measure does not become a weak spot in your home's security.

Your standard rim locks are not good enough security. Better lock options include:
- Long throw gate locks
- Hasp and staple locks (work with a padlock)
- Mortice deadlock

Chapter 2 – The Indoor Defense

Once you have made it unlikely that intruders can get into your outdoor space, focus on securing your indoor space. After all, if intruders are insistent or suave enough to bypass these barriers to entry, the outdoor measures that you have installed will only serve as delays rather than deterrents. Ways that you can decrease the chances of intruders breaking into your home include:

Securing Your Doors

Typically, when we think of nefarious characters breaking into our homes, we picture them climbing in through windows, but the truth is that most of them access our homes the same way that we do—through our doors. Therefore, one of the first means of fortifying your home includes securing your doors.

As mentioned before, get rid of flimsy, standard locks. Intruders will easily pick them. Use enhanced locks instead. They are not so easily picked, as they use multiple locking mechanisms. While it might be annoying to carry multiple sets of keys, you can have the peace of mind that your home is unbreachable.

The material that your door is made up of should also be a consideration. Exterior doors should be made of aluminum, steel, fiberglass, or top-quality wood so that they can stand the highest impact force. Reinforce that protection by installing strike plates and door jammers.

Doorframes and hinges also need to be well-installed and of sturdy quality. No matter how strongly made the door is, a well-placed kick can displace it if it is not held up by a strong wooden frame. The same applies to the hinges.

Lastly, remember that no amount of security will help you if you forget to lock your doors. Remind yourself and encourage other family members to periodically check if those have been locked.

Securing Sliding Glass Doors

Not only is the material of glass doors easy to break, but they also have other weak spots. The locks can be easily picked. If an intruder is crafty enough, this person can learn how to simply lift the glass door right out of the tracks from outside of your home.

If replacing the glass of your French doors is not an option, there are inexpensive solutions that you can implement to make them more secure. Such measures include the installation of:

- Track locks that prevent the sliding door from being opened.
- Sliding door loop locks that jam the door and prevent it from being opened.
- Sliding door locks, which are installed on the top and the bottom of the door to prevent unwanted entry.
- Double bolt locks that prevent the door from being lifted out of its tracks.

Be mindful that none of the measures above prevent the glass from being broken. You should consider applying a security window film or external security door, such as a metal gate, to increase security.

Securing Your Garage

In addition to keeping the garage door closed and locked when no one is around and installing lighting in and around your garage, additional measures that make them less likely to be broken into include:
- Ensuring that the landscape features are appropriate and do not hinder the view of the property or serve as a hiding space for criminals. Plant small, thorny shrubs near garage windows to prevent this from being a means of entry.
- Do not keep high-value items in the garage. If you absolutely must, ensure that the view into the garage is obstructed.
- Be smart with how you store an automatic garage door opener. If intruders get access to this, they have unhindered entry into your home.
- Keep your garage emergency release out of plain view.

Securing Your Windows

Depending on the type of window, they can either be broken or pried open by intruders. The first measure of safety that you can implement to lessen the likelihood of this happening is to ensure windows are closed and locked, especially when you are not at home. Next, you can consider the following tips to beef up the security surrounding your windows:
- Keep your blinds or curtains closed after nightfall. This will prevent criminals from learning exactly who is at home and what they can expect to find inside.
- Use curtains or blinds to hide the contents of your home and garage to not tempt criminals to break in.
- Use tempered glass on your windows to make them less breakable.
- Install security bars or window grills to secure windows. Only do this if you have other emergency exits in your home.
- Secure horizontal sliding windows with wooden dowels placed in the lower track.
- Consider installing window locks, such as latches and sash locks. Just like with security bars and window grills, only do this if you have other emergency exits in your home.
- Consider installing rollaway security shutters. These are not only great for keeping intruders out, but they also serve as a safety measure during storms.
- Install security window wells to protect basement windows.

When you are implementing the safety measures to secure your windows, be mindful that windows can also serve as a means of escape during an emergency, such as a fire. Find a balance between security and safety.

Installing Security Alarms and Cameras

The installation of home security alarm systems gives you an added layer of protection that comes in the support of the installation company. When you get a monitored service, the system automatically alerts the alarm company when something is amiss. The company then contacts local authorities, who will come to check on the situation that prompted the alert.

Depending on the type of system that is implemented, loud noises can be emitted when motion is detected or a sensor is tripped. This serves as a deterrent, as most criminals will flee from the sound.

Be mindful that system batteries can run out of power quickly when the power is out. Therefore, it is best not to depend on the system solely. Try to have a backup power system in case there are extended power outages. Also, criminals are becoming increasingly tech-savvy and are finding ways to bypass such systems. Therefore, if this is a security measure that you do implement, ensure that you choose a system and a service that are reliable and not easily hackable.

Security cameras are a great way to keep track of the activity around your home and its surroundings while you are away, especially in conjunction with a home security system. In this day and age, you can do this from anywhere in the world using your smartphone, as the footage streams via wireless internet. The best part is that you can learn to install these on your own and do not have to rely on a security company to do it. Placing security cameras in plain sight or having a sign that states that the property is being monitored by security cameras can also act as a deterrent for criminals.

Getting a Guard Dog

Having a guard dog serves multiple purposes in deterring intruders. The deep, threatening sound of barking can scare away would-be trespassers. The sound of barking draws attention and can call other people to the scene of a crime in progress. In more unrestful times, dogs can help you hunt for food and serve as a defense mechanism by keeping attackers from physically getting to you.

Again, if for whatever reason you cannot get a dog to guard your property, there are more practices that you can implement to make it seem as though one is present. There is a device called barking dog alarm that uses motion detection to activate the sound of barking. This sound becomes more intense the more motion is detected.

Chapter 3 – The Deterrents

We have identified possible weak spots that can attract intruders to your home. Now let's focus on placing active deterrents around your home that make them want to stay clear.

In addition to the deterrents mentioned at the weak points above, additional measures that can be implemented include:

Home Security System

Home security systems are meant to protect your property from intruders and burglars. An effective home security system also protects your home from fires and other environmental disasters. Many home security installation companies also provide professional monitoring services that let you know if there is a problem, such as a burst pipe or a gas leak. They can even provide medical emergency relief. The additional benefit that I love is that they allow you to monitor your home even while you are away, such as on vacation or at work, through video and audio surveillance.

Unfortunately, scammers are everywhere, so if you are looking into getting a home security system, be sure to do your homework to get a reliable and reputable company to do so.

Warning Signs

Let's think about the psychology behind this deterrent. If we ever see a bio-hazard sign or one that says an electrocuting fence, we will stay clear of that area. Why? Because we do not want to get hurt or place ourselves in unnecessary danger. You can apply the same psychology to protect your home with a simple sign. It makes intruders stop and think twice about the risk they take by entering your home.

One of the first possible signs that you can get is one that announces that you have a home security system. You can do this even if you do not have one installed. What an intruder does not know will keep him or her away.

Another possible sign for you to hang up is one that says, *"Beware of Dog"* or *"Guard Dog on Duty."* This sign has a double function. First, it acts as a deterrent to thieves, as they would immediately imagine a dangerous dog patrolling the property and be more likely to stay away. Second, it protects you from legal charges brought against you if the intruder does not heed the sign and gets injured by your dog. After all, this person noted the sign and still chose to trespass. You can also hang the sign up even if you do not have a dangerous canine patrolling your property, as it makes intruders think twice about coming onto your property.

One of my personal favorites is the sign that says, *"Nothing Inside Worth Dying For."* Even though there is no clear threat, it sends a clear message to intruders that you are active in protecting your property and that gaining entry will not be an easy feat. Most criminals are looking for an easy score.

Lastly, the good ole fashion *"No Trespassing"* works. Just like the sign mentions, it does not state a specific threat, but it is implied, and psychology works just as well as physical threats in most situations.

Before we move on, let's address where on your property you should place these signs. While this is not a strict and hard rule, it is best to prioritize placing your signs on the right side of your property because most people rely on their right hand as their dominant hand. As a result, most human beings tend to move in that direction first.

Evidence of a Guard Dog

As mentioned before, having a dog to guard your premises is a wonderful deterrent to intruders. If you cannot afford a guard dog, or simply do not want the responsibility, you can still trick intruders into believing you do have one. Such misleading evidence includes leaving a bowl of water or a dog bone in clear sight. Such a tactic is particularly helpful in times of crisis when looters are looking for easy scores.

Anti-Climb Spikes

If it is legal in your area, consider placing anti-climb spikes on the sides and fences of your property to deter intruders from gaining entry to high points. Because they can pose a possible danger to human life, anti-climb spikes are highly regulated, hence the need to seek out the legality of it in your area.

Bulletproof or Tempered Glass

Bulletproof glass is quite an expensive option for protecting your windows and doors, but it is well worth it if you can afford it. Not only will bulletproof glass keep the occupants of the home safe from flying bullets, but it also protects from impacts.

On the less expensive side of things comes tempered glass or window film. When installing tempered glass, ensure that it is installed on the inside of the window frame or that the edges are caulked to the frame. These security measures come in handy in extreme situations, such as violent looting. Criminals tend to have even fewer scruples then and are not above using bodily harm and brute force to get their way. Tempered glass is made out of multiple layers of plastics and adhesives that hold glass together even when they have been impacted. This slows criminals down and also keeps the people inside safe by protecting them from the sharp, flying debris.

A Licensed Gun

It is sad to say, but we live in dangerous times, and the multiple threats that we face from other people do not look to be going away anytime soon by the simple fact that we are facing human nature. Facing a crisis only increases the danger, and one of the most effective ways that you can protect yourself, your family, and your home is with a firearm.

A handgun is the most basic type of firearm that you can get. It comes in many types, such as a double-action revolver, semi-automatic pistol, smoothbore pistol, and single-shot pistol. These firearms are convenient because of their small size and weight. They can be held and used with one hand. Handguns are used mainly in self-defense, and their small size allows them to be easily concealed on your person.

Apart from your basic handgun, options when it comes to protecting your home with a firearm include a rifle, which is a long-barreled gun that is bigger and heavier than a handgun. These are more suitable for hunting and is a heavier form of self-defense.

If you do opt-in to getting a licensed firearm to protect yourself, your loved ones, and your property make sure you always know where it is and how to use it. If you are not carrying the firearm on your person, be sure to store it in a safe or similarly secure area that is not within easy reach of others, especially young children. Remember that, while these tools are meant to keep you and your loved ones safe, they can also be dangerous to the people you want to protect if not handled with care and caution.

Home Traps

One of the most famous examples of home traps being highly effective comes from the movie *Home Alone* where little Kevin delayed burglars from entering his family home. Home traps serve to delay intruders. Often, they are effective in keeping such dishonorable individuals trapped until authorities can get to the property and ensure everyone is safe

Here are a few home traps that I recommend installing on your property:

Tripwire

This is one of the most well-known yet effective types of home traps. It makes use of a stretched cord, or wire, that is placed close to the ground and attached to an alarm. The premise is that the intruder will step hard against the wire, or cord (hopefully, tripping in the process), to pull it so that the alert is activated. This type of trap is so effective that it is still being used in the military and police today.

You can install tripwires in your home quickly and effectively. There are kits that can be purchased at stores but, in a pinch, all you have to do is get a rigid wire, such as a fishing line, to set up the perimeter that you would like to keep secure from intruders. Install this away from where your family, friends, and loved ones might become injured.

Feather Spear Trap

This type of trap has deep roots and was historically used to keep wild boars out of human-occupied areas. It is just as effective in keeping intruders out of your home.

The feather spear trap uses a primitive but complex system made up of wooden spears attached to a tripping device created from a piece of fixed wood and a wire. Such a trapping device is best confined to being used in the wilderness because of how effectively dangerous they are.

Paracord Snare Trap

Just like the feather spear trap, this trap is used for hunting and catching small game. It is made of a noose tied to a stick. This stick is anchored to the ground. The premise of this trap is that it catches animals around the neck or body. Struggling against the cord used in this trap only makes it tighter. Because of how extremely effective this trap is, it is illegal to use in many states in the US. However, it is great for survival situations and, therefore, handy for every prepper to know.

Explosions Simulator

This is a deterrent security measure, as it simulates the sound of an explosion. This sound can be as loud as 120 decibels; loud enough so that intruders will not know what hit them and be driven away in the confusion. It is even loud enough to cause bodily damage. Exceeding the 120-decibel limit ventures into illegal territory.

The sound, accompanied by small amounts of fire and smoke, is triggered by a built-in electronic timer. You can create your own explosion simulator by modifying a sprinkler valve.

We have nailed down protecting your home, person, and valuables. Now we move on to giving you a better understanding of medicine for preppers and the basics of natural medicine in a world without pharmaceuticals. Turn the page.

Book 9:

The Defense: Healing Yourself

Garlic. While many people might not know that it is considered a vegetable and not a herb, we all know that it makes our food taste great. For as long as garlic has been noted for all the wonderful things that it does to our taste buds, it has also been known for its medicinal advantages. There have been many historical references to the medicinal good that garlic has done for entire societies.

The Dark Ages (also called the Middle Ages) is known for many things, such as violence, but did you know that people who lived in this era from 476 AD to 1000 AD used garlic liberally to treat and heal themselves?

Hippocrates of Kos, who also went by the name Hippocrates II, was born in 460 BC and died in 370 BC. He was a well-known physician of the Greek classical era and was renowned for his contribution to the world of medicine. He was a firm advocate for the many advantages of using garlic to fight many diseases and illnesses, and as a purgative agent.

Hippocrates was not the only Greek to hail garlic as a medical saver. The Greek alchemist, Theophrastus (371 BC to 287 BC), also advocated for the health benefits of garlic. Even early Olympians ate garlic before competing in games to increase their strength. Greek soldiers also ate garlic for the same reason.

Ancient Egyptian slaves used garlic to stay strong and fight off sickness, also. Do not quote me on this, but it might be because of garlic that we have the pyramids erected today. To back my opinion, to increase the strength and stamina of labor building the pyramids, these people were "paid" in garlic.

This was not the only mention of garlic as a medical remedy in ancient Egypt. The Codex Ebers (1500 BC), which is an ancient Egyptian medical document, prescribed garlic to treat several different ailments, including parasites, insect infestations, general feelings of unwell, and abnormal growths.

Ancient Romans used garlic to treat cardiovascular gastrointestinal and musculoskeletal problems, as well as epilepsy. Dioscorides (40 AD to 90 AD), a chief Roman physician, describing garlic's benefits, cited, "cleans the arteries and opens up the mouths of the veins." Another Roman physician, Pliny the Elder (23 AD to 79 AD), recommended garlic as a treatment for 23 illnesses, including toothaches, sore throat, earaches, tapeworm, insomnia, epilepsy, poor circulation, hemorrhoids, and animal bites from scorpions and shrews, to name a few.

Ancient Chinese used garlic to remove poison from the body and to treat male impotence, headaches, and fatigue, in addition to using it as a food preservative.

Ancient Indians used garlic as an aphrodisiac and to treat arthritis, heart disease, rheumatism, coughs, fevers, and more. They also used it to heal cuts and bruises.

Even after the Dark Ages ended and we saw the birth of the Renaissance period, there are mentions of garlic being used in old and new ways medicinally. There are even mentions of garlic's medicinal properties in both the Bible and the Talmud. I really can go on and on about the many healing benefits of using garlic, a plant found so abundantly on our planet, noted from even ancient times.

While the people of these ancient periods revered garlic for all of its medicinal purposes, we in the modern age have stepped away from just how much of a great impact this one vegetable can have on the human body. It is never too late to embrace the benefits of this plant, though.

Garlic is just one of the many species of plant life that we can use to keep healthy and return to good health after we have fallen sick. This chapter gives you insights on using natural remedies like garlic to not only stay healthy during normal living but also, how they can come in clutch to make you survive during times of crisis.

The Medicinal Introduction

Natural Medicine and its History

Natural medicine far exceeds the use of just garlic. Natural medicine has been placed in the media spotlight as of late, so you might have heard the term being used quite liberally. But, what is natural medicine and what place does it have in the modern world?

Let's start by defining what natural medicine is. Also called herbal medicine, natural medicine is a form of alternative medicine that focuses on the body's capabilities of healing itself with natural intervention rather than the use of pharmaceutical drugs, vaccinations, medical operations, and other modern medicines. Natural medicine is a branch of naturopathy, which is the practice of using lifestyle routines, like diet, acupuncture, homeopathy, and more to stay fit and healthy.

Natural medicine revolves around the idea that we are self-healing devices that have great vitality. Pure natural medicine practitioners believe that all parts of the body are interconnected, so when we look at ensuring that the body is optimally functional overall, we become self-healing organisms. The aim of following natural medicine traditions is to achieve balance within their bodies rather than relying on modern medicine, where it is largely believed that symptoms of illnesses and diseases are suppressed rather than addressed.

There are strong beliefs that drive the popularity of modern medicine today, but what are its origins? Even before herbal medicine pioneers of the Middle Ages and the Classic Greek era, there are records of natural medicine being used. In the age of the Neanderthal around 100,000 BC, early homo sapiens used plants to treat illnesses. Plants used for medicine among their many functions, like chamomile and yarrow have been found in the remnants of teeth of these people after their remains were uncovered by scientists.

The practices of Ayurvedic medicine, based on an ancient Indian medical system that dates back to 2500 BC, relied on natural and holistic approaches to maintaining and up-keeping both physical and mental health. The traditions of their use of natural medicine, as well as that of other cultures, have been passed down from generation to generation.

Fast forward several thousand years and we as a global society have moved away largely from such natural systems. Why, when there was so much evidence of their effectiveness when used correctly? There are two main reasons. First, Western culture and sciences rely heavily on written documentation (and rightly so) to pave the way forward. The practices of natural medicine were mostly passed down through the generations orally. As such, there was not much of a foundation to build natural medicine on before. Second, the Industrial Age made it so that most human activities were commercially driven. Therefore, even medicine became big business as pharmaceutical companies built empires founded on people being sick. Whether we like to believe it or not, pharmaceutical companies do not make money from us being healthy and illness-free. They certainly do not make money from us being able to simply walk to our gardens and pick the cure to our ailments right there. Most people were content to use modern medicine, as it offered what looked like quick fixes.

However, over time, the dangers of modern medicine revealed themselves. The focus is on treating sickness rather than maintaining health holistically, so the use of modern medicine has led to the death of many people every year. Many of those deaths can be linked to the side effects that pharmaceutical drugs have. With more and more horror stories emerging of people's experiences with synthetic drugs, people started looking for another way, a more *natural* route.

There was a long period when natural medicine was largely forgotten by the masses. But the search for a better means of being and keeping healthy has brought a global spotlight to alternative medicine; natural medicine being one of them.

Chapter 1 - Benefits of Natural Medicine

If there weren't so many advantages associated with using natural medicine, it would never have made it out of Medieval Times to become a sought-out way of maintaining health. So, what is in it for you to practice natural medicine? These benefits include:

- Anyone of any age with any level of health can practice natural medicine. From babies to the elderly, natural remedies are effective. This is also the case when people have preexisting conditions, like fatigue or gastrointestinal problems that are typically triggered by the use of pharmaceutical drugs.
- The emphasis of natural medicine is placed on treating your body as a whole. All too often, pharmaceutical drugs isolate and suppress the symptoms of one ailment *after* it has become a problem. Practicing natural medicine focuses on maintaining optimal health of the whole body with healthy lifestyle practices that upkeep the mind, body, and soul. Suppression is not the aim of natural medicine in the eventuality of sickness. Rather, it focuses on treatment so that the problem is nipped in the bud.
- There are almost no side effects associated with the use of natural medicine. With proper research on what plants are best for treating certain illnesses, most people walk away from using natural medicine with no side effects, which are common with the use of pharmaceutical drugs.

But what do all these benefits mean for you as a prepper? Let's dive into that discussion next.

Chapter 2 - Natural Medicine for Preppers

In times of crisis, access to medical services and even pharmacies can become barred. Just like with food, it is best to have a stock of medicine on hand that allows you to treat illnesses that you or your loved ones might already suffer from and common ailments that might arise. You need to create your own backup pharmacy in your home in case medical systems fail you when you need them most.

Natural medicine can not only be your fallback plan, but it can also be incorporated into your lifestyle. Every day, more and more viruses and bacteria become resistant to pharmaceutical drugs. As a prepper, this should be a concern for you because as the Covid-19 pandemic has shown, viruses and other pathogens pose as great a threat to human life as any man-made or natural disaster. It should also be of concern the political favoritism that is shown to pharmaceutical companies, as they suppress the bright news about natural medicine. All too often, healthcare is governed by the propaganda of politicians rather than healthcare professionals.

In Eastern cultures, such as the Chinese culture, natural medicine is used in tandem with modern medicine. The two co-exist rather than exist in competition as it does in Western culture. I have not written this book to persuade you toward adopting a way of life that is completely reliant on natural medicine. Rather, I aim to help you see that you can use both to your advantage no matter the times. You can prep your home with the pharmaceutical drugs you deem safe to use and fall on natural medicine in times where these might not be available or you simply want to upkeep your health holistically.

Even many experienced preppers underestimate the value of being prepared for medical emergencies ahead of time. What if you become injured or sick when healthcare services are not available? What if medical and pharmaceutical supplies are cut for your access or there is a shortage? What if modern medicines expire without you realizing and there is no means of restocking? How do you survive and care for your family in those and like instances? These are questions you must answer before it becomes a reality. That is the only way you will be adequately prepared.

Adequately prepared preppers fall back on natural medicine for many reasons, including:
- It does not belong to any one person or corporation. Anyone and everyone has access to natural medicine and can use it.
- Practicing natural medicine is sustainable over the long haul. The only limitation that you have to maintain a supply of natural medicine is the growing condition of plants. Even that limitation can be nullified with proper planning and the use of preservation methods. You do not have to be a slave to whether or not pharmacy shelves are stocked.
- It is easy to learn the ins and outs of natural medicine without formal education. Additionally, learning is fun and provides constant mental stimulation as there is always something new to learn.

- Natural medicines can be bartered for other items if necessary. Medicine is always in demand, and if social norms and constructs fall apart during a crisis, you can be assured that you have something valuable that other people would happily trade other valuable items, like food, for.

Natural medicine works. Make it work for you during everyday life and the tide turns to direr waves.

Chapter 3 - FAQs About Preparing for Emergencies with Natural Medicine

You might have a few questions at this point about how to prepare your own in-home pharmacy in case of emergencies. Before we move on to the how of creating such, let's address some of the most frequently asked questions about how to ensure you have an adequate supply of medicine for emergencies.

How much medication should I store for emergencies?

This question is difficult to answer, as every individual and every family has different medical needs. The answer lies with you. For you to answer it, you need to determine what your and your household's medical needs are and then calculate the amount of medication necessary to care for those needs in a worst-case scenario for at least one year. I like to have enough over-the-counter on hand for at least two years. Once you calculate the amount necessary, stock a little bit extra. Prescription drugs are harder to stock for long periods but try to have a month to two months stocked to back up what you use regularly.

Just like with stocking food, I adopted a first in, first out methodology of using medication. Pharmaceutical drugs pack an expiration date, so you might be tempted to stock excessive amounts. However, this can lead to wastage if you do not use the medicine fast enough or you get over the condition that requires its use. Another handy note is that, just like food, medications are typically still good after the expiration date on the bottle has been reached. The expiration date simply states the date it is best to be used by. Still, it is great to ensure you get medications as far from the expiration date as possible.

The expiration date will be of little consequence if you do not store these meds properly. Leave these meds in the original packaging they came in unopened. Do not place them in the bathroom medicine cabinet (or anywhere else in the bathroom really) because this environment is humid and has too high of a temperature. Instead, store extra medication in a cool, dark place with an environment similar to where you store your emergency food

What do I do if anyone in my family has allergies or special needs?

The medical needs of every household are different. There may be persons in yours who have special requirements when it comes to medicine. To determine these needs (and to calculate the amount of medicine you need to stock for emergencies), answer the following questions:
- Are there infants in your household? If yes, what child-formulated medications do you need to stock?
- Does anyone in your household have medical allergies? If yes, what alternative solutions should be stocked to cater to these?

- Does anyone in your household suffer from seasonal allergies? If yes, what medications are needed to deal with the symptoms?
- Does anyone in your household have chronic medical conditions? If yes, what medicines are needed to handle this?
- Does anyone in your household require medicine for pain management? If yes, what quantities of which drugs are needed for this management?

The answers to these questions will allow you to calculate the amounts you need for both over-the-counter and prescription meds. Knowing this is not just useful for emergencies but also for everyday use.

Are there any medications that I or my family members specifically need?

While every household has different needs, there are a few over-the-counter medications that most families find useful to stock. I will provide a list of these toward the end of this part of the book.

What chronic conditions should I be aware of?

Chronic conditions are those that are considered to last a year or more and require a person to seek ongoing medical attention. Chronic conditions tend to limit a person's activity daily. Some of the most common chronic conditions that preppers need to be aware of include:

- Kidney Disease
- Heart Disease
- Stroke
- High Blood Pressure
- High Cholesterol
- Respiratory Disease
- Alzheimer's Disease
- Diabetes
- Cancer
- Arthritis

If you or any or members of your household suffers from any of these chronic conditions or others, you need to ensure that medication is on hand for at least one year because of the long-standing nature of chronic conditions.

Book 10 – All About Natural Medicine

Before we move on, I need to explicitly state one thing - **Herbal medicine is not meant to substitute medicine prescribed by medical professionals.**

This book was not written as an advocate to replace modern medicines. Always remember that natural medicine is meant to support modern medicine and not as a replacement.

Being Safe While Using Herbal Medicine

Natural medicine is not without risk, especially when it is used improperly. To minimize the possibility of you harming yourself if you decide to incorporate herbal medicine into your lifestyle or during an emergency, here are a few tips:

- Be well-informed before using any herbal medicine.
- If you're buying any natural supplements or medications, read the product descriptions and the ingredients included to avoid allergic reactions and scams.
- Be mindful that the anecdotal proof supporting herbal medicine is not scientific proof.
- Be mindful that different people get different results from using natural medicine.
- Discuss natural options with your doctor before taking them.
- Avoid using herbal medicine if you are pregnant or breastfeeding unless it is approved for that specific purpose.
- Avoid giving small children herbal medicine unless it is approved for that specific purpose.

Chapter 1 - The Tools of Natural Medicine

Now that you are mindful of the risks versus the rewards of using herbal medicine, here are the tools that you need if you decide to forge ahead:

Solvents

These are the substances, typically a liquid, used to dissolve other materials. In this case, they act to extract the compounds that have healing qualities from plant parts. Examples of solvents include oil carries like coconut oil and almond oil, high-proof alcohol, gin, vodka, vinegars, honey, and glycerin. The solvent used depends on the recipes used to develop the healing solution.

Wax and Butter

These are used to create healing creams, salves, and body butters. Wax options include soy, candelilla, and beeswax. Butter options include koku, shea, cocoa, and avocado.

Storage Containers

These are needed to store the finished product. Mason jars are a common option, but other options include jars, tins, and glass bottles. Ensure that they are sterilized before use.

A scale

A common kitchen scale will do. This is used to ensure precision during the preparation process.

Mixing Bowls

This is to mix the ingredients to be prepared.

Saucepans

This is required for recipes that need cook time.

Measuring Utensils

These are also used to ensure precision during preparation as waxes, solvents, herbs and more need to be added in specific qualities to get a safe and usable end product. Items in this category include measuring cups, graduated cylinders, and measuring spoons.

Cutting Utensils

Items in this list include scissors, shears, and knives. They are needed during the harvesting of the plant parts and, sometimes, during the preparation.

Hand Lens

This allows you to make informed decisions when foraging and harvesting plants. They magnify the small parts of plants for proper identification.

Notebook

This is useful for many reasons including jotting down recipes, thoughts, plant identification features, and any other item that you find useful as a herbalist.

Chapter 2 - Herbal Remedies Using Common Spices

Did you know that your spice cabinet could be a means of keeping you from getting sick and aiding you to feel better faster when you do get sick? Here are some options and just a few of the medicinal applications:

Cumin

This spice promotes proper digestion, improves blood cholesterol, promotes weight management, and is a great source of iron.

Black Pepper

This helps improve digestion and clear congestion.

Nutmeg

This spice aids in improving heart health. It also has strong antibacterial properties.

Cloves

This spice is an anti-inflammatory and an antioxidant. It is also an anticancer agent that helps slow bone and cartilage loss caused by arthritis. Cloves can also help relieve the pain of toothaches.

Cayenne

This contains a compound called capsaicin which is a muscle pain reliever. This and other compounds in cayenne pepper also help treat the symptoms of the common cold, the pain of arthritis, nerve pain, and shingle pain. Cayenne is also an anti-inflammatory and an antioxidant.

Cinnamon

Sprinkling some of this spice on your oatmeal or toast helps control blood sugar levels. Cinnamon is also an anti-inflammatory and antibacterial agent. It is also an antioxidant.

Cardamom

This is a diuretic and antioxidant. It is also an anticancer agent that helps with digestive and oral health.

Common Medicinal Herbs

Just like spices, some herbs are a common find in many households that can also be used medicinally. Some of them include:

Coriander

This herb aids in improving digestion by treating irritable bowel syndrome and other gut issues. Consuming it can also treat anxiety. It is an antioxidant.

Thyme

This is an anti-inflammatory agent that also relieves congestion.

Garlic

We will discuss this herb in *Part 4*.

Turmeric

We will discuss this herb in *Part 4*.

Ginger

We will discuss this herb in *Part 4*.

Mint

This highly nutritious herb improves brain function, gets rid of bad breath, relieves indigestion, and decreases the pain associated with breastfeeding.

Chapter 3 - Useful Ingredients for Making Homemade Herbal Remedies

Apart from those listed throughout the content above, some ingredients you made need to develop your own home remedies include:

- Sugars, to sweeten teas, wines, syrups, and more. Substitutes for this may include maple syrup and honey.
- Salt, like table salt, sea salt, Epsom salt, or sodium chloride. These may be used to preserve your natural medicines.
- Bentonite clay, which is used to aid natural remedies in pulling toxins out of the body.
- Essential oils to control the scent of some of your herbal medicines. You may add peppermint oil to homemade mouthwash or lavender oil to creams.

Book 11 – Growing Your Own Herb Garden

You can, of course, source some herbs from stores but the most assured way of getting the herbs you need for specific ailments is to create your own herb garden. Doing so is not difficult at all. It includes these simple steps:

Identifying the Herbs that Grow Well in Your Area's Climate

This is the planning stage of developing your herb garden. To do this, you need to know what your needs are, what remedies can be easily created in your home and thus, which herbs need to be planted to create them. Create a list based on this.

It is ideal to match your herbs to the location. Most herbs do well in certain climates. At this point, it is time to do some research on which of the herbs on your list are feasible for growing in your area. Cross out any that do not apply, and then you can proceed to the next step.

Locate Your Garden Zone

While some people may have the luxury of yard space for planting a herb garden, not everyone is privy to such. However, even if you live in a small apartment, you can create a herb garden as long as you get creative.

Research the avenues for making your space work for you as where there's a will, there is a way. For example, you may have to utilize patio space or the window ledge in your kitchen.

Map Out Your Landscape

Map out how you will plant the herbs in your garden in the space available to you. You need to account for the space between plants. Begin by drawing a rough map of the space with measurements.

Determine the Amount of Each Herb You Need

Based on the types of herbs that you have chosen and the amount of space available to create your herb garden, calculate the number of each herb you will need. This will help you determine the number of seeds, shoots or cuttings that you need to source for planting. From then on, it's all about caring for your herbs and maintaining the ideal growing conditions to get the best end product.

Book 12 – The Natural Medicine Remedies

Whether you source natural medicine from your garden or forage in the wild, there are a few options that are proven to work for the majority of people. You can harness the power of natural medicine for yourself with the popular options below.

Chapter 1 - A Natural Medicine List

Chamomile

What does it look like?

This plant has a striking resemblance to daisies with flowers containing white petals surrounding a yellow, cone-shaped center. Its leaves are fern-like and light green. The plant grows to about 3 feet.

Where can you find it?

Different species of this plant react to different environments but, in general, this plant likes fertile, well-drained soil and partial shade.

What parts should be used and for what purpose?

The leaves of this plant can be used to make tea and extracts that help relieve stomach pain, diarrhea, constipation, nausea, upper respiratory infections, and urinary tract infections. The leaves can also be developed into topical compresses to treat wounds.

Chamomile is generally safe to use, but stay away from it if you have had allergic reactions to marigold, ragweed, or daisies, as you are likely to react similarly.

Cinquefoil

What does it look like?

This plant is a member of the rose family. It is typically identified by the five leaflets that make up its compound leaves. Be mindful that you may come across species of this plant whose compound leaves number three, seven, or even more leaflets.

This plant is perennial with five-petaled flowers. The flowers are usually colored yellow, but you may also come across red or white varieties. These flowers produce fruits that look like dried strawberries. Because of their shrub appearance, cinquefoil can be used for landscaping.

Where can you find it?

This plant grows best in open forests, wet mountain meadows, on the banks of rivers and streams, and on damp rock ledges. It also loves full sun and moderately acidic soil. It is easy to locate in northern parts of the US and around the Rocky Mountains.

What parts should be used and for what purpose?

The flowers, roots, and leaves of this plant are used medicinally. These medicinal properties are extracted through creating a tincture (dissolving the plant part in alcohol), tea, or decoction (boiling or heating the plant part to extract essence) from these parts.

Also going by other names, like goose grass, five-fingered grass, cramp weed, potentilla, and shepherd's knot, this plant is used to treat premenstrual syndrome (PMS) symptoms, the pain of menstrual cramps, sore throats, sealing hemorrhages, for reducing fevers and more.

The diluted tincture can be gargled as a mouthwash.

Columbine

What does it look like?

This is a perennial herb with a branching stem that grows to about 5 feet tall. Its leaves are basal (forming from the base of the stem) and hairy on the underside. Its flowers range in color from white to purple and blue. These flowers bloom in May and contain five petals. They have backward projecting spurs that are about ¾ inch long.

Where can you find it?

This plant grows best in full to partially shaded areas with mid-range soil moisture conditions. As a result, they are found frequently on wood borders and on riverbanks. In the US, they are common finds in the north, east of the Rocky Mountains.

What parts should be used and for what purpose?

The leaves and stems of this herb can be used to make medicines that treat ailments such as gallbladder disorder, the symptoms of scurvy (a disease developed from a vitamin C deficiency), jaundice, intestinal issues, skin rashes, and more.

Echinacea

What does it look like?

A relative to sunflowers and also called a coneflower, echinacea is a plant that normally achieves a height of 5 feet and has a straight stem. Its leaves are narrow and lance-shaped. They are also toothed, dark green, and have a few white hairs along the upper surface.

Its flowers range from pink to purple in color. Florets grow around a cone that contains several seeds. The cone has prickles.

Where can you find it?

These plants are native to North America in places like the Rocky Mountains, in open prairies, and wooded areas. States where this plant grows naturally include Alabama, Georgia, Oklahoma, Kansas, North Carolina, and Missouri.

The flowers bloom in mid-summer for about 1 month.

What parts should be used and for what purpose?

Several parts of the plant can be used medicinally, including the flower petals, the leaves, and the roots. These parts are typically used as a tea or supplement, but they can also be turned into topical creams.

The primary medicinal use of this plant is to treat and prevent the common cold. However, it can also be used to treat toothaches, sore throats, an upset stomach, and treating wounds and burns.

This plant is only for short-term medical use, as side effects like stomach pain, nausea, and rashes can be experienced over long-term use.

Elderberry

What does it look like?

Elderberries are woody shrubs. Their bark is smooth and green. Occasional white spots will be spotted along the bark. As the elderberry ages, the bark turns brown. The shrub can grow up to about 4 feet.

Its leaves are light green, pointed, serrated, and grow to as long as 5 inches. The single-stemmed plant produces white flowers that grow in clusters. Its berries are purple.

Where can you find it?

These plants grow in moist forests, along the banks of marshes and streams, and areas where the soil has a lot of drainage. Still, this plant can tolerate dry soil, so it is well spread across the continental United States. States where you might find elderberries include Texas, Florida, and Minnesota.

What parts should be used and for what purpose?

The fruits of this plant have medicinal properties when they are cooked. It can also be made into tea or syrup. The product relieves colds, constipation, viral infections, headaches, toothaches, and nerve pain. This primary function is to relieve the symptoms of the cold and flu.

Never eat the stems, seeds, leaves, or roots of this plant. Be mindful that this plant looks like water hemlock, which is poisonous. Note the picture below. The major difference between these two plants is that water hemlock grows in the water while elderberries are tolerant of dry conditions. Another difference is the structure of their leaves. While elderberries' leaves grow opposite each other, the leaves of water hemlock have an alternating pattern.

Feverfew

What does it look like?

This is a flowering plant with the Latin name *febrifugia*, which translates into the meaning "fever reducer." It grows to about 1.5 feet tall and produces small daisy-lookalike flowers. As such, they are reminiscent of the blooms that chamomile produces so the two plants are often confused. They are white with bright yellow centers and grow in clusters at the top of the stems. The leaves are light green and hairy. The leaves may look more yellow than green.

Where can you find it?

This plant is native to Asia but grows well in many parts of the world, including the USA. It loves cooler climates and tends to be found in abandoned fields and gardens, along roadsides and trail edges. The weedy plant loves partial shade.

What parts should be used and for what purpose?

The main medicinal use of this plant is given away by its name. It reduces fever. Additionally, it helps treat migraine, is a pain reliever, has some anticancer effects, treats common cold symptoms, reduces inflammation, and helps treat rosacea, to name a few medicinal effects.

The flowers and leaves of this plant, both fresh and dried, have medical purposes and are the most commonly used in such a capacity. Extracts of this plant also serve the same duty, as all parts of the plant that are above can be used.

Foxglove

What does it look like?

This plant is typically seen from June to September and grows up to a height of 4 feet. Lots of insect life, like honeybees and moths, are found around this plant, because its bright purple-pink flowers are highly attractive. The tube-shaped blooms may also be yellow, red, lavender, or white. The flowers are clustered and often marked with spots on the insides of the petals.

Its large, flat leaves are oval-shaped and hairy. The edges are toothed. They form at the base of the stems.

Where can you find it?

This plant loves temperate climates and can be found in woodlands, sea cliff sides, moors, and hedge banks.

What parts should be used and for what purpose?

All parts of the plant that grow above the ground can be used medicinally. This plant is toxic if used in large doses, but small amounts can be used to strengthen heart contracts and treat heart rhythm abnormalities. In fact, this plant is used to make the pharmaceutical drug called digoxin, which is used to treat heart failure. Talk to your doctor before using this natural medicine.

Garlic

What does it look like?

This pungent vegetable is nutrient-packed and often a part of some of our tastiest recipes. Garlic grows from a bulb, and each bulb contains several cloves. Roots grow downward from the bulbs to anchor the plant into the soil, and shoots grow upward to provide the parts of the plant that we see. The leaves of wild garlic are vibrantly green and pointed with a smooth edge. Delicate white flowers bloom in clusters above this.

Wild garlic grows to a height of about 1.5 feet. It is closely related to onions, and they give us a similar strong scent. This plant tends to grow abundantly with large numbers of wild garlic in the same spot.

Where can you find it?

This plant grows best in full sun, in slightly acidic to neutral soil. Garlic grows dormant in colder weather but grows well in late September to November and can be harvested the following summer. Garlic can, of course, be found in gardens, but it also grows in woodlands and other areas with damp soil in temperate climates.

What parts should be used and for what purpose?

Garlic is associated with many medicinal uses, including treating high blood pressure, relieving digestive problems, as a diaphoretic (to induce sweating), as a diuretic (to increase urine flow), as an antiseptic, and many more. There are even compounds in wild garlic that have been found to reduce stress.

Wild garlic goes by many other names, such as bear's garlic, wood garlic, gypsy onion, and wild leek. The cloves, leaves, and flowers have been found to have medicinal uses.

Ginger

What does it look like?

A herbaceous plant, ginger is a shoot that arises from an irregular-shaped, underground stem, which has a strong aroma. The rhizomes can be dark yellow or different shades of brown.

Its leaves can grow to as long as 12 inches long. They grow in an alternate arrangement. It produces flowers that range in colors from purple to yellow-green. The flower looks like a pinecone and grows to about 3 inches long.

Where can you find it?

Used as a spice and food, this plant grows well in well-draining, moist soil, in partially shaded areas. This plant is native to Southeast Asia but can be cultivated in the conditions mentioned.

What parts should be used and for what purpose?

The rhizome of the plant is used for its medicinal properties. A rhizome is an underground stem to which shoots and roots are connected. This rhizome can be used fresh or dried and made into a capsule and tea. Ginger is used to treat nausea, migraines, colds, colic, flatulence, and high blood pressure. Large doses of ginger can lead to diarrhea and heartburn, so limit the amount that you use.

Gingko

What does it look like?

Also called ginkgo biloba, this plant has male and female trees. The difference is that the male trees produce larger flowers compared to the inconspicuous nature of the female trees' flowers. Because their leaves turn an attractive golden color in fall, these trees are often used in landscaping. The branches spread out in a crown, adding to the beauty of the tree.

Their leaves are also unique with a fan shape and round lobe. The veiny structures are green and grow to as long as 4 inches.

These trees bear round fruit that looks like mirabelle plums. The fruits have a diameter of about 3 inches. They are green when ripe and turn yellow by the time they fall off the tree. The fruits tend to have an unpleasant smell.

Where can you find it?

Native to China, this plant has been cultivated in the USA.

What parts should be used and for what purpose?

The leaves of this plant are used to make teas and tinctures, which are medicines created by dissolving the plant's part in alcohol. It is used to treat several ailments, like heart disease, sexual dysfunction, and dementia

Ginseng

What does it look like?

This is a leafy bush that grows to an approximate height of 15 inches. Its stalks produce leaves in sets of threes, and these then branch out into clusters of leaflets.

The plant normally produces flowers between its second and fourth years of growth. They are elliptical, ranging in color from green to white, or green to yellow. The small flowers are produced in clusters between 30 and 50 strong on one stalk.

Where can you find it?

The natural habitat of this plant is woodlands like those found in Central and Eastern North America. States where this plant grows naturally include Alabama, Maine, Indiana, Rhode Island, Pennsylvania, South Carolina, and Missouri. Wisconsin is the top producer in the USA.

What parts should be used and for what purpose?

The roots of this plant are frequently used medically to increase immunity, energy levels, and brain function. They are used to reduce inflammation, as well. They are dried then ground into a powder or steeped to make tea.

GoldenSeal

What does it look like?

This is a perennial plant from the buttercup plant family. It grows to about 12 inches tall. It has a yellow rhizome that is filled with golden sap. The plant produces dark green leaves that are palmate-shaped. The leaves have a double serrated margin. A mature goldenseal plant has two or more erect stems.

Its greenish-white flowers bloom around early May, depending on the exact location, and develop into a berry-like fruit that turns red in July and contains black seeds.

Where can you find it?

This plant loves to grow in moist semi-open areas, so it is a common to find in open woodlands, forested slopes, and along river and stream banks. The plant grows widely in the US and can be found in states such as Arkansas, Minnesota, and Georgia.

What parts should be used and for what purpose?

This plant's roots are commonly used to treat ailments, such as mucous membrane problems, pink eye, urinary tract infections, and skin problems. It also has anti-inflammatory and antibacterial properties. Its dried roots are also used to create supplements in many states in the US. The herb can be used as a diuretic, a laxative, or a tonic.

Lady's Mantle

What does it look like?

This is a perennial plant that grows in clusters. Its leaves are circular with scalloped edges. It grows leaflets with silvery undersides that are silky to the touch. The leaves are deeply dissected and palmately lobed.

The plant produces clusters of yellow-green flowers. These flowers bloom from June to September.

Where can you find it?

This is an easy-growing flowering plant that is found in many habitats, such as along roadsides, in parks and yards, along streams and river banks, on grazing land, in meadows, etc. It prefers to grow in full or partial shade with medium moist and well-drained soil that is acidic to neutral in pH.

What parts should be used and for what purpose?

Lady's mantle is used to mend torn tissues, such as eardrums, muscles, tooth extractions, hernias, and wounds in general. It is also thought to cure anxiety and insomnia. It can be applied internally and topically. This plant is largely geared toward promoting good female health. It is made into a tonic to promote female reproductive system health and can also be used to tame excessive vaginal discharge, irritation, and infection. It also contains elements that relieve female ailments, such as the pain of menstrual cramps.

The leaves, flowers, and roots are used to facilitate these medicinal wonders through the development of extracts and gels from these plant parts.

Lavender

What does it look like?

This shrub-like plant is a perennial known for its strong scent and the therapeutic effect it has. It grows to an approximate height of 3 feet and produces flowers that range in color from purple, lavender, light pink, and white. The flowers are upright spikes that grow in whorl clusters and create an attractive array that attracts birds, insects, and humans alike. They bloom from June to August.

Its leaves are gray-green, and they assemble to form a compact plant. They are narrow and oblong, growing to a length of about 2 inches. They have a spiral arrangement and are packed densely together.

Where can you find it?

This plant originated from the Mediterranean region and grows well in temperate climates. The plant loves plenty of sunlight and well-drained, sandy soil with alkaline to neutral pH. It can grow well even in dry conditions, as it is highly resilient.

What parts should be used and for what purpose?

This plant treats headaches, fungal infections, acne, digestive issues, stress, and eczema, in addition to having antiseptic and anti-inflammatory properties, which is useful in treating insect bites and minor burns.

The flowers and their buds are used to gain these medicinal benefits. They are developed into essential oils and tea.

Lovage

What does it look like?

This is a perennial plant from the carrot family that can grow up to 6 feet tall. Also called mountain celery, this plant produces dark green leaves that resemble those of parsley. They have a glossy texture.

Lovage's flowers are umbel-shaped and yellow.

This plant has a yeast-like, celery scent.

Where can you find it?

This plant prefers the growing conditions of shading areas, as well as rich, moderating stony soil.

What parts should be used and for what purpose?

This plant is packed with various B vitamins, as well as vitamin C. It contains compounds with antioxidant and anti-inflammatory properties. It has a variety of medicinal uses, such as treating an upset stomach, relieving skin irritation, as an eye bath to relieve sore eyes, to get rid of the pain of menstrual cramps, as well as treating bronchitis and ulcers.

Relief from these ailments is gained from making infusions, lozenges, vinegars, tinctures, and essential oil from its plant parts. The leaves can be applied directly to the skin to clear up acne, rashes, and psoriasis. Apart from the leaves, the roots and stems are used medicinally.

Milk Thistle

What does it look like?

This plant has sharp points on the leaves, flowers, and stems, and it grows to about 3 feet tall. It produces a distinct flowerhead, which is bright magenta or purple. The flowerheads have a fleshy, thick spine bract that protrudes from the base of the head. Each flower can produce about 200 seeds. The flowers are long and wide, and they bloom from June to August.

The leaves are oblong with shiny edges. They grow in an alternate pattern and have milky white veins.

The stems and branches are thick, hollow, and ribbed. The plant is sparsely branched.

Where can you find it?

This plant prefers rocky, dry soil in sunny or partially shaded areas along roadsides, in ditches, on cow fences, and pastures.

What parts should be used and for what purpose?

Also called holy thistle, it treats a variety of ailments, such as diabetes, upset stomach, heartburn, gallbladder problems, menstrual pain, hangover, and even some types of cancer, to name a few. All parts of the plant, such as the leaves, flowers, fruits, and seeds, can be used to extract the compounds that facilitate these medicinal advantages. They are dried to create infusions (plant parts steeped in water until the flavors and oils are absorbed), powders, teas, tonics, and tinctures. Remember that the plant is protected by spines. If you harvest this plant, protect yourself from injury and wear appropriate gloves.

Be mindful that milk thistle should only be taken in small doses, as larger doses can cause gastrointestinal issues, such as constipation, nausea, vomiting, diarrhea, and abdominal bloating

Pennyroyal

What does it look like?

This plant is a member of the mint family and has a spearmint aroma. It is a perennial herb that produces small, lilac blooms at the ends of its stems. Also known as mosquito plant and pudding grass, it is a creeping plant with gray-green leaves.

Where can you find it?

It grows in woodlands, floor, and seasonally wet areas, along marshes and stream banks, and ditches across the US. It likes sunny to partially shaded conditions and moist, well-drained, acidic soil.

What parts should be used and for what purpose?

The leaves and oils extracted from this plant are used medicinally. They are used to treat pneumonia, common cold, fatigue, flatulence, liver disease, stomach pain, indigestion, and as an insect repellant.

Primrose

What does it look like?

This plant produces flowers that can be blue, red, yellow, purple, white, or orange. They bloom in the springtime and have an umbel shape. Some species of primrose grow flowers that form in clusters while others produce a single flower on a stem.

Primrose leaves are dark green and are tongue-like, with hairy, wrinkly undersides. They form a rosette at the base of the plant.

These are short plants that grow to about 4 inches tall.

Where can you find it?

This plant thrives in partially shaded conditions with moist, well-drained, acidic, clay-quality soil. They are often found in grasslands, woodlands, and hedgerows. They are found most plentifully in the Western USA.

What parts should be used and for what purpose?

Medicinal uses can be derived from making parts of this plant into teas and essential oil. Such parts include the leaves and flowers.

Primrose is used to treat eczema, asthma, attention-deficit/hyperactivity disorder (ADHD), headache, nerve pain, whooping cough, hepatitis B, premenstrual syndrome (PMS), breast pain, menopause symptoms, and more.

Rosemary

What does it look like?

A member of the mint family, this is a fragrant shrub with green, needle-like leaves. It can grow as tall as 6.5 feet. The leaves are narrow and curve downward. They have fine hairs on the underside and are shiny on top.

It produces blue, purple, pink, or white flowers. They have protruding stamens.

Where can you find it?

This plant is native to the Mediterranean region and thrives in more extreme conditions of high temperatures and sunlight. Rosemary is frequently found in coastal areas.

What parts should be used and for what purpose?

The oil extract and leaves of this plant can be used to relieve muscle pain, relieve headaches, improve memory, increase blood circulation, increase hair growth and prevent hair loss, and to treat indigestion. They can be developed into essential oil, creams, and ointments.

Sage

What does it look like?

This is a perennial plant that grows to a height of about 2 feet. It produces wrinkly, ovate leaves that have a range of colors, like white-green and gray-green. They can grow to 3 inches long. They grow in an opposite pattern and are pointed.

Its flowers are tube-shaped and resemble spikes. They can be red, pink, purple, or white. They produce nutlet fruits.

Where can you find it?

This plant thrives in growing conditions where there is medium to full sun exposure, the soil is well-draining and acidic to neutral in pH. It also loves sandy soil. Note that this plant is tolerant of dry conditions. This plant is often found near limestone. US states where this plant is frequently found include Colorado, Nevada, Wyoming, Idaho, Montana, Utah, North Dakota, and South Dakota

What parts should be used and for what purpose?

The leaves of this plant can be used to produce teas and essential oils. These leaves help treat stomach pain, flatulence, loss of appetite, diarrhea, heartburn, and bloating, to name a few.

St. John's Wort

What does it look like?

This is a herbaceous plant with a woody stem and opposite leaves. The plant produces small, bright yellow flowers that grow in clusters at the end of its branches. Each flower is about half an inch and has five petals that have small, black dots at the margins.

Where can you find it?

This plant grows best in wet soil but can also be found in dry, gravelly areas. Look for St. John's wort in fields, pastures, and sunny locations. The US states where St. John's wort has been spotted include California, Idaho, Oregon, and Montana.

What parts should be used and for what purpose?

The flowers of this plant are used to create teas, extracts, and capsules that can be used to treat insomnia and lung disease. They can also be used to treat wounds.

Do not use this natural medicine if you take an antidepressant, certain kinds of cancer treatments, blood thinners, some pain medicines, and birth control.

Saw Palmetto

What does it look like?

This is a palm-like tree that grows to over 10 feet tall and spreads out wide. It is characterized by a leaf arrangement that looks like a fan. These leaves are thorny and pointed, growing along the plant's stem. Most species of this plant produce green leaves, but there are also blue-silver and silver varieties. Its branches produce small, yellow-white flowers that turn into small, yellow berries. The berries turn black as they ripen.

Where can you find it?

While this plant loves full sun, it will grow in shade, as well. It benefits from moist soil but is drought tolerant. This plant is a common find in Florida.

What parts should be used and for what purpose?

This plant is used to enhance hair growth, increase fertility, boost libido, treat enlarged prostate, and improve urinary function. It also has anticancer effects. The fruits of the plant facilitate these and more medicinal improvements. This can be taken as a supplement, a tea, an oil extract, or even eaten whole.

Sorrel

What does it look like?

This is a flowering plant used as both a veggie and an herb. It grows to about 4 inches tall. Sorrel develops as a rosette with small white flowers. The flowers are round with purple veins.

Sorrel's leaves are rounded lobes and look like clovers.

Where can you find it?

This plant can be found naturally in grassland areas but is often cultivated in controlled habitats. Other natural habitats include open woodlands, meadows, and fields.

What parts should be used and for what purpose?

This is an anticancer plant and is used in the herbal treatment of cancer. Other uses include as a diuretic, anti-inflammatory agency, antioxidant, pain reliever, and antibacterial agent. The leaves, fresh and dried, are used medicinally. They are turned into syrups, infusions, and teas.

Turmeric

What does it look like?

A member of the ginger family, turmeric is an herb that has medicinal properties in addition to infusing cooking with wonderful flavor. The plant grows to about 3 feet tall and produces yellowish-white flowers that grow from a spiky stalk. The leaves are dark green and oblong. They grow to about 5 inches long.

Where can you find it?

Turmeric is a cultivated plant that is typically grown indoors or in regulated greenhouses. The plant grows well in shade and soil that is enhanced with organic matter.

What parts should be used and for what purpose?

The dried rhizome of the plant is used to create turmeric powder. The active compound in turmeric, called curcumin, helps relieve pain and reduce inflammation in addition to other medical aids. This aid typically comes in the form of a supplement or as a spice. Therefore, you can intake this natural medicine by using it in cooking.

Turmeric should only be used in small doses, as high concentrations can lead to headache, diarrhea, and skin irritation.

Valerian

What does it look like?

This is a flowering plant. The look of this plant tends to induce a feeling of calm and serenity with its umbrella-shaped head of clustered white flowers. The flowers can also be purple or pink and have a sweet smell. The plant grows to about 3 feet, has a hollow, strain stem and dark green, appointed leaves.

Where can you find it?

This plant is native to Europe but is found in other parts of the world, as well as in several states across the US. While this is a great garden plant, it also grows well in damp grasslands, forest edges, along river banks, and in meadows, fields, and abandoned areas.

What parts should be used and for what purpose?

The roots of this plant are used medicinally to treat heart palpitations, tremors, restlessness, anxiety, insomnia, stomach cramps, and headaches. This is done by drying the roots to make tea and capsules.

Vervain

What does it look like?

This plant grows upright to about 4 feet tall. It produces opposite branches and leaves. The leaves are lobed and toothed with the upper leaves being significantly smaller. Its flowers are pink or lilac and small. They grow in a spike-like, tubular shape to about 5 inches in length. The flowers grow into red-brown fruits.

Where can you find it?

This plant loves full sun conditions but will grow in partial shade. It also grows best in well-drained, acidic soil. Sandy or loamy soil is best for it. It is found commonly in meadows, pastures, riversides, and thickets.

What parts should be used and for what purpose?

The medicinal uses of this plant include its antitumor and antimicrobial properties, in addition to its treatment of anxiety, insomnia, depression, gum disease, and infections. All the parts of the plant that are above ground during its flowering period are used medicinally. They can be developed into a decoction or poultice (a moist mass of plant material applied to the body externally). They can also be eaten raw.

Wintergreen

What does it look like?

This is an evergreen shrub that has aromatic qualities, produced from the leaves. It is low to the ground, developing from creeping stems. Its leaves are ovate, dark green, and shiny. They grow to about 1 inch long and have hairs along the slightly toothed edge.

Wintergreens produce bell-shaped flowers that dangle from the leaf axils. They can occur in singularity but also in small groups. The small flowers are waxy white, growing to as long as .5 of an inch.

The flowers develop into small berries. They start light green and mature to a bright red color.

Where can you find it?

This plant is found in the eastern part of the US in habitats like hardwood forests. It prefers acidic, coarse, moist, well-drained soil. It tolerates partial shade.

What parts should be used and for what purpose?

The leaves of this plant are used as teas, infusions, decoction, and poultices, and created into an oil extract to be used medicinally. They are used to treat the common cold, tapeworm, stomach aches, rheumatism, kidney issues, and headaches. The poultice is applied to rashes, bruises, and wounds.

Woodruff

What does it look like?

This is a creeping perennial herb that grows to about 12 inches tall. It spreads about 18 inches and also goes by the names wild baby's breath and sweet-scented bedstraw, among many.

The leaves of this plant are lance-shaped and dark green. They smell like fresh hay when crushed and smell so good that the dried leaves can be found crushed and sold commercially as perfumes and in sachets.

The flowers smell just as good with a nutty, vanilla aroma. They are white and star-shaped. They grow in clusters and bloom in April and May.

Where can you find it?

Native to Northern Asia, Northern Africa, and Europe, this plant grows well in well-drained, moist soil but can survive in dry soil. It also tolerates a range of soil pHs from alkaline to neutral to acidic. It appreciates partial and full shade. In the US, it can be found in rocky forests, near streams, and generally avoid open vegetated spaces.

What parts should be used and for what purpose?

All the parts of the plant that grow above the ground are used medicinally. The fresh leaves can be applied to cuts and wounds to heal. A decoction can be used to cleanse the liver and aid digestion. Teas and oil extracts can also be made to assist with righting a variety of other ailments, like preventing and treating heart, lung, gallbladder, and urinary disorders.

Yarrow

What does it look like?

As a member of the aster family, this plant is another daisy lookalike. Its flowers are dome-shaped and grow in clusters. They are white, typically. In the wild, occasionally, pink blooms might be spotted. Cultivated yarrows may have red, pink, orange, or yellow flowers. The flowers bloom anywhere from April to October. The plant grows year-round through.

The plant can grow as tall as 3 feet and produces aromatic, fern-like leaves. Its stems are grooved and the plant produces a fresh pine needle scent.

Where can you find it?

This plant is commonly found in grassland areas, open forests, moist meadows, along roadsides, gardens, and disturbed land. It is native to temperate regions.

What parts should be used and for what purpose?

All parts of this plant above ground can be used medicinally. Uses include treating the common cold, diarrhea, loss of appetite, hay fever, fever, and gastrointestinal (GI) tract discomfort. Among its other medicinal uses, the fresh leaves of yarrow can be chewed to relieve the pain of a toothache.

Because of its relation to the aster family, yarrow can also be confused with many other plants, but one you should be wary of is poison hemlock, which is toxic to humans. Note its picture below. The biggest difference between these two plants is that the poison hemlock's leaves are more frilly and its flowers are umbel.

Chapter 2 - The Ailments and Their Medicines

There are a variety of aches, pains, and discomfort that we suffer from daily. An upset stomach, a headache, cramps, and so on. You do not have to grit your teeth and suffer from these commonalities because you are dealing with the fallout of a disaster. Not if you have a well-stocked home pharmacy and natural medicine to aid you. Even items in your pantry can come in useful for making you feel right as rain. This section covers simple remedies for common maladies.

Headache

We have mentioned a variety of over-the-counter medications that you can take for headaches, such as acetaminophen. However, if you suffer from headaches frequently, taking such pharmaceutical medications regularly can lead to more harm than good, as it can damage your heart, liver, kidneys, and intestines.

It is better to take an alternative that does not have so many side effects, and magnesium glycerin is your solution. This is a supplement that is created from magnesium and glycine. Glycine is an amino acid that will bring magnesium to the areas where it is needed most for fast action. If you suffer from occasional headaches, taking a 200 mg to a 400 mg tablet will give quick relief.

Nausea and Sickness

Ginger increases gut motility and aids in digestion. It also serves as an antacid that soothes an upset stomach. Peppermint also serves the same purpose.

Luckily, both of these natural remedies are easy to incorporate into your food. They can be cooked with dishes, added along with other ingredients to make smoothies, made into teas, and used as a tincture. They can even be of great use as essential oils.

Be mindful that if you suffer from nausea and upset stomach regularly, this is indicative of a more serious underlying issue. As such, you may want to consult with a medical professional.

Acid Reflux

It seems like there is nothing that apple cider vinegar will not cure, and acid reflux is on that list. This remedy, which is found in most cupboards around the United States, helps to regulate blood sugar levels and develop conditions where good bacteria thrive in the gut. Such an environment is effective for relieving heartburn.

You can also relieve heartburn with the use of digestive bitters.

Constipation

The supplement magnesium citrate is great for relieving acute cases of constipation. All you need is a 200 mg to 300 mg pill before bed. There are also powdered versions that can be stirred into water.

If you suffer from chronic constipation, this may be addressed by modifying your lifestyle to remove food intolerance, up the amount of fiber in your diet, and remain hydrated.

Sore Muscles

A natural medicine to relieve muscle pain and soreness is arnica. This is a meadow flower. You do not have to have this plant growing in your own garden to make use of it, as it can be found over the counter as a cream or gel. The only potential side effect associated with such creams and gel is a mild allergic rash.

Joint Pain

Curcumin is the bright yellow chemical that gives plants, like turmeric, their vibrant color. The chemical is also an antimicrobial, antioxidant, and anti-inflammatory agent. These anti-inflammatory properties help ease joint pain.

Luckily, curcumin can be found as a supplement. Taking 500 mg twice daily can go a long way in relieving your joint pain. You can get an additional boost of pain relief by incorporating turmeric into your diet.

Earache

Earaches are not a malady limited to suffering babies. They are a common symptom among adults, as well, especially during times of the common cold and flu infections. Antibiotics are the normal pharmaceutical prescription to treat earaches, especially in young children, but they typically only offer pain relief and do not treat the underlying cause. Additionally, intestinal disorders are a possible side effect of their use.

You can relieve mild infections with natural ear drops containing the herb garlic mullein. The herb has anti-inflammatory properties, thus decreasing the swelling in the area. This helps relieve the pain and increase the speed to getting rid of the infection.

Sleeplessness

Instead of suffering through another sleepless night, you can use essential oils made from lavender to induce you into a state of sleep that is deeper and more restful. You can add this to a diffuser or keep it in a light bulb next to your bed. You can increase the effectiveness of this by adding a few drops of this oil to an Epsom salt bath.

The Flu

The primary way of quickly recovering from the flu or even the common cold is to increase your fluid intake. Giving your body the hydration that it needs flushes out pathogens from your system.

You can supplement this action with the addition of vitamin C to your diet. Taking vitamin C shortens the lifespan of your flu or cold. It also helps boost your immune system health.

Honey is a microbial and antiviral solution that can shorten this life span, as well. Add it to your favorite herbal teas, like gingers and echinacea, both of which aid with treating the flu and cold.

Runny Nose and Congestion

You do not need a drugstore decongestant to flush out a runny nose and cure congestion. In fact, I would say stay away from them if you can, as potential side effects include a rise in blood pressure. They can also create a dependency.

A simple way to flush out your sinuses is by using a saline solution, which is simply a saltwater solution that you can create at home. All you have to do to create your own saline solution is to add 1 cup of distilled water to a clean container. Next, add 0.5 tsp salt and 0.5 tsp baking soda. Mix to dissolve. Pour the solution into a medical syringe or squeeze bottle. Insert the tip into your nostrils. Gently squeeze so that the saline solution goes out of your mouth or the other side of your nose.

Sore Throat

Hot tea with honey and lemon is the go-to for healing a sore throat the natural way. Lemon juice gives you a boost of vitamin C while honey has antimicrobial and antifungal properties.

Certain teas have immune-enhancing properties, and antimicrobial and antiviral agents, that lessen the lifespan of a sore throat. Such teas include green tea and elderberry tea.

You can strengthen the effect of this combination by taking extracts of goldenseal and echinacea.

Cough

Inhaling steam does wonders for relieving a hacking cough. Ideally, you can get this effect from going to a sauna, but you can do this in the comfort of your home by running a hot shower or filling a bowl with hot water and draping a towel over your head as you lean over the bowl. Add a few drops of eucalyptus oil for even faster relief.

Body Aches

If you suffer from body aches frequently, this may be a sign that you need more sleep. Sleep is restorative and helps the body heal. Inadequate amounts of sleep do not allow this, so body pain is one of the outcomes.

The solution? Develop good sleep hygiene and hit the hay at a consistent time that allows you to get 7 to 9 hours of sleep every night.

Chapter 3 - The Herbal Medicine Dosage

Dosage of natural medicine matters just as much as it does with pharmaceutical drugs. Taking too little means that the desired effect will be missed. Taking too much means risking being overdosed and all the ill consequences that come with that. Getting that dosage right can mean the difference between life and death.

This section serves as a general guide to dosages for different age groups. Before we get into the specifics of dosages, here are a few guidelines for administering natural medicine:

- Do not give babies below 6 months natural medicine.
- Pregnant and breastfeeding women should not take natural medicines unless advised by a medical professional.
- Do not double doses.
- Do not take more than one herbal medicine at a time, as you do not know how these items will react with each other.
- If you notice any adverse reactions to taking herbal medicine, immediately stop and seek medical help.
- Do not take natural medicine for more than 2 weeks without professional medical advice.

Now that we have the formality out of the way, here are the dosage recommendations for a few types of natural medicines:

Tinctures

Adults are considered 12 years and older. The adult dosage recommendation is 2 droppers. This is about 60 drops. Based on this, the recommendations for other age groups are:

- 9 to 12 years – 30 drops / about 1 dropper
- 6 to 9 years – 24 drops
- 4 to 6 years – 15 drops / ½ dropper
- 2 to 4 years – 10 to 12 drops
- 1 to 2 years - 6 to 8 drops
- 9 months to 12 months – 4 to 6 drops
- 6 to 9 months – 3 to 4 drops

Teas

1 cup is the adult recommendation when natural medicine is administered this way.

Moving down the age ladder, the dosages are:

- 7 to 11 years old - 2 tablespoons
- 4 to 7 years old - 1 tablespoon

- 2 to 4 years old - 2 teaspoons
- Below 2 years old - ½ to 1 teaspoon

The same dosage recommendation applies to infusions.

Book 13 – The Ultimate Prepper's Medicine List

This section gives a thorough list of items that you should stock to develop your own at-home pharmacy.

Chapter 1 - Over-the-Counter (OTC) Medication

Stocking over-the-counter medication is easier and tends to be less expensive than stocking prescription medication. Some of the best over-the-counter medications that you can keep in your emergency stash include:

Ibuprofen

Ibuprofen is used to relieve pain, as a fever reducer, and to treat inflammation. As a result, it is useful in treating menstrual cramps, arthritis, arthritis pain, back pain, sore throat, sinus pain, headaches, muscle strains, and more. Ibuprofen can be effective when used in conjunction with acetaminophen to relieve severe pain, such as that associated with the removal of a wisdom tooth. Examples of common ibuprofen products include Advil and Motrin.

Naproxen

This type of medication is similar to ibuprofen and is also effective at relieving pain, reducing fever and treating inflammation. The difference is that its effects tend to last longer (about 12 hours). A common naproxen is Aleve.

Aspirin

Aspirin is effective at reducing swelling, reducing inflammation, treating pain, and reducing fever. In special cases, it can be used as a blood thinner to prevent stroke, heart attacks, and blood clots. However, it must be used in small doses in such instances. Get a professional to give you advice on this. Children under the age of 12 with a fever should not be given aspirin, as there is a risk of developing Reye's syndrome. Popular brands of aspirin include Ecotrin and Bayer.

Acetaminophen

Unlike ibuprofen, naproxen, and aspirin, acetaminophen is not an anti-inflammatory drug. However, it is great at reducing pain and fever. A popular example of acetaminophen is Tylenol.

Diphenhydramine

This is an antihistamine used to treat the symptoms of allergies, hay fever, hives nausea, itching, and respiratory infections. In some instances, it can also be used to treat insomnia and anxiety. Benadryl is an example of inexpensive diphenhydramine.

Loperamide

This is used to treat gastrointestinal issues, such as intestinal cramping and diarrhea. A typical example of loperamide is Imodium.

Polyethylene Glycol 3350

This is used as an osmotic laxative, to relieve constipation and as a stool softener. This is helpful to keep on hand because dealing with disasters can lead to the development of stress and a change in your diet. These conditions can lead to bowel and other digestive issues. An example of this is MiraLAX.

Glycerin Suppositories

This is another medicine that helps to deal with constipation. I keep this on hand in case polyethylene glycol 3350 is not effective.

Pseudoephedrine

You might be acquainted with the popular brand of this type of medication called Sudafed. It is a decongestant that helps relieve congestion along with the symptoms of hay fever, allergies, bronchitis, the flu, and the common cold.

Fexofenadine Hydrochloride

Allegra is an example of this medication. It is an antihistamine that helps relieve allergy symptoms. It is often taken along with pseudoephedrine for maximum effectiveness.

Meclizine

This is an antiemetic drug that helps relieve motion sickness, dizziness associated with vertigo, vomiting, and nausea. It can also help some people who suffer from insomnia and anxiety. Examples include Bonine and Dramamine.

Famotidine

Pepcid is an example of this drug. It is useful in treating ulcers, acid reflux, and heartburn.

Bacitracin Ointment

This is an antibiotic ointment used to treat lacerations, stings, insect bites, and abrasions, as well as superficial bacterial skin infections typically associated with an infected wound. Baciguent is an example of this drug.

Stocking prescription drugs is not as easy as it is with over-the-counter medications. However, it is doubly important that you stock prescription medications because of the hindered access to them. You may be able to do this by speaking to your health care provider and explaining to this person why you see the need to have extra prescription medication on hand. In such cases, the medical provider may be able to fill your prescription for up to periods between 30 and 60 days. If this is the case, be sure to rotate your supply and follow the professional recommendations. Also, remember to refill your prescriptions as early as possible.

Chapter 2 - The Medical Kit

Along with stocking medications as needed, it is also necessary to develop an adequately supplied medical (first-aid) kit. This will allow you to swiftly handle minor accidents and injuries. Just like with medications, your first-aid kit should be stored in a cool, dry place that is out of the reach of children. The best thing about a medical kit is that it can be taken with you anywhere, so medical help is available to you at any time.

Be sure to include items that are needed for the specific needs of your family members in your first-aid kit. For example, keep glucose tablets in your kit if any member of your family suffers from diabetes. However, there are a few universal items that every medical kit should have as part of its contents. Items that should be stocked in your medical kit include:

Gauze

This is a thin and translucent material used for dressing wounds. It is highly absorbent, so can soak up blood and stop the flow. Gauze is also sterile and keeps wounds from getting infected. To keep that level of sterility, wash your hands with antibacterial soap or use hand sanitizer before handling it.

Gauze comes in a variety of sizes. Keep several sizes stocked in your medical kit. Choose the size that is appropriate and wrap the wound in it after the wound has been cleaned. Keep it secure with medical tape, another item that should be in your first-aid kit.

Remember that gauze is a temporary solution if someone is seriously injured. Get medical help as soon as possible, in that case.

Bandages

For less serious accidents and smaller injuries, bandages are used instead of gauze. Therefore, bandages are perfect for instances like a scraped knee or a cut on your fingers.

Applying a bandage is simple. Clean your hands first by washing your hands with antibacterial soap or using hand sanitizer. Clean and disinfect the wound with an antiseptic solution followed up with an antibiotic ointment. Apply the bandage and ensure it is firmly stuck to the skin surrounding the wound while not being too tight.

Antibiotic Ointment

This item is necessary for treating open wounds, like cuts. It is necessary to prevent these wounds from getting infected and becoming a bigger problem. To use them, all you have to do is apply a small amount of antibiotic ointment to the affected area before dressing with a bandage. Along with Baciguent, more common over-the-counter antibiotic ointments can easily be accessed, including Neosporin, Bacitracin, and Polysporin.

Antiseptic Wipes

A wound needs to be sterilized before it is treated or you risk infection. That is the purpose of having antiseptic wipes in your medical kit. These wipes contain alcohol or hydrogen peroxide, typically. They are the disinfecting agents. You should also have these items stocked in your medical kit to treat larger wounds. Add cotton buds to that list and you have a makeshift antiseptic wipe.

Anti-itch Cream

An itch can arise from many instances, like coming into contact with poison ivy or being bitten by a bug. Having an anti-itch cream, like calamine lotion or 1% hydrocortisone cream, comes in the clutch in those cases. Hydrocortisone cream is better for getting rid of the itch associated with bug bites, while calamine lotion is better for treating contact with poison ivy.

Be mindful that more severe reactions cannot be treated with topical items like these. Be sure to get medical assistance in this case as soon as possible.

Multi-Tool

As the name suggests, a multi-tool houses several built-in tools in one device. These built-in tools can pull out splinters, cut gauze and bandages as needed, and so much more.

Antihistamine

This is a must for any household where one or more of the occupants suffers from allergic reactions, such as seasonal allergies. Apart from the typical antihistamine, like Benadryl, if any of your household members have more serious allergic reactions, be sure to also keep an epinephrine pen in your medical kit.

Hand sanitizers

The best way to keep your hands clean for treating wounds and handling sterile items, like gauze and bandages, is to wash your hands with antibacterial soap. But often, during an emergency, we aren't close to a clean, running water supply or antibacterial soap. The next best thing to do is use hand sanitizer to sterilize your hands. Therefore, this is a must-have for your first-aid kit.

Instructions

Sometimes someone else might have to administer aid using your medical kit. Sometimes you might forget the special instructions for using certain items in this kit. Sometimes, you might have to rely on a child to give care using the items in the kit. In those instances, or any other of uncertainty, detailed instructions need to be provided so that care remains consistent with good health practices. A guide with step-by-step instructions for using each item should be included in your kit.

In the same breath, it should be said that each member of your family needs to know how to use each item in the first-aid kit, including kids. Routinely act out emergency scenarios with members of your household to ensure they know how to react in these cases.

The next part of this series will go deeper into living off the grid and how you can disappear from the world to protect yourself and your family.

Book 14:

The Lifestyle: Living Off the Grid

When most people hear the phrase "off the grid," the immediate imagery that comes to mind is roughing it. While that might be one meaning applied to the phrase, living off the grid is more than that, as it means different things to different people. This book in the series explores those different meanings and how you can safely and happily adopt such a lifestyle, if that is your choice.

To depict that living off the grid means different things to different people, here are a few people who did just that. We start with the story of Keith Callahan and his wife. The two lived in Western Washington. They started building a shed on their property, which was on 5 acres. The shed was supposed to serve as a place to store material possessions while they traveled abroad. When they returned to the US, they moved into the shed and simply never left.

When they first made the move, they were truly roughing it, as the shed had no electricity, running water, or insulation. But the upside that made it worth it for the couple was that they were not being rained on by a cloud of debt. So, they upgraded the shed to make it comfortable for them. They installed a solar electric system and gained hot, running water through a harvesting system installed on the roof. Their garden also housed their shower and bathtub. Along the way, their son was born in 2010. The family remained disconnected from the world, as most people have it and off-the-grid living works for them.

Our next story features a woman called Kirsten Jacobsen, who moved to New Mexico to help build her own Earthship home. Earthships were the invention of an architect called Michael Reynolds. His vision was to build sustainable homes created from recycled materials, like aluminum cans and tires. Kirsten finished her

Earthship home in 2006. Even though the home does not have any utilities, it has a heating and cooling system. Kirsten even added "more modern-looking finishes and other things, like stainless steel, a clear glass bottle-brick wall, and bamboo floors in the bedroom."

Much like the Earthships, the Dancing Rabbit EcoVillage of Missouri produces homes largely based on natural building techniques that leave a far lesser environmental footprint compared to your traditional modern home. The homes are made with reclaimed or sustainable obtained wood, straw bales, and natural plasters.

The architectural designer, Alex Whitcroft, moved to the region to learn these techniques and became one of the approximately 60 residents in 2011. Dancing Rabbit has integrated wind turbines and solar arrays to be even more eco-friendly and less dependent on the "grid." While some of the homes look like what you would expect of a normal American home, they use approximately 90% less electricity.

Living off the grid does not work for everyone, but these stories show that it is a practice that can be just as comfortable as the life we have become accustomed to as part of the rat race. Better yet, you can customize the type of living to mean what you want it to be.

By the time you read the last page of this book, you will have weighed the pros and cons of this type of living, what it really entails, and how you can efficiently make a go at it.

The Off-Grid Living Introduction

To understand what it means to live off the grid, you first need to familiarize yourself with what the grid is. The grid is a reference to an electrical grid, which is an electrical system that delivers power to both commercial and residential properties. Living on the grid means a dependency on other entities, such as the electrical company, for comfortable living. If you have to get really philosophical about it and get down to the bones of it, it is about a dependency on things exceeding the electrical company. This is about a dependency on other entities for water, sewer, and other basic necessities facilitated by utility services.

Living off the grid is about removing that dependency and becoming disconnected from these entities. But, does lack of dependence translate into primitive living? It does not. Living off the grid means what you want it to mean. If you want to adopt a more primitive lifestyle, you can. If you want to incorporate modern conveniences, then you can do that, as well. If you want to find a medium in between, that is also an option. Therefore, to one person, living off the grid may mean that you are disconnected from a traditional electrical supply. To another person, it might mean being disconnected from all utilities. Some people might step this up a notch and live a completely self-sufficient life, going so far as to be independent of public sources of food or housing. There is no black and white vision of what it means to be off the grid. I cannot stress this enough—it is what you want it to be. So, if you take nothing else from this section, know that living off the grid is about being disconnected from the electrical grid. Everything else is customizable to suit your taste. You create the rule book for your experience.

Chapter 1 – Tackling the Myths about Off-Grid Living

There are a lot of rumors going around about what it means to live off the grid, you might be overwhelmed by what others have to say and not sure what to believe. This section was written to clear the fog by tackling the common myths surrounding the living practice. We will tackle each one by one and state whether they are true or not with the evidence that supports the side of the scale that has been tipped.

Myth #1: You need to be self-sufficient

Self-sufficiency in this case refers to producing all your food on your own. This myth is a misconception.

There are plenty of people who live off the grid and do runs to the supermarket and grocery stores to do bulk buying. While it would help you have means of obtaining the food that you need, such as herb, fruit, and vegetable gardens, your level of dependence on food obtained from a third party is your standard to set. You might even develop a barter system with your neighbors who have gardens and livestock. If you ever end up with an excess of an item, you may swap that item for another with them and vice versa.

Myth #2: You have to be experienced in farming

Speaking of gardens, do you have to have farming experience to make it off the grid? This question has arisen because we see lots of stories of people swapping city life for off-the-grid living and seemingly set up huge farms in the blink of an eye. While that may be the reality for some people, it is not feasible for everyone. The great news is that, even if you do not have a green thumb, you can live off the grid. This is a false myth.

Again, it would be handy to expand these skills. With books, videos, courses, and the internet at our fingertips, you can learn the art of gardens and even raising livestock. Just take it one step at a time and find joy in learning. So, instead of building a barnyard to raise livestock, start by raising a few chickens. Instead of trying to cultivate an entire acre of land with fruits and veggies, start with a kitchen garden. Start with learning those activities that are actually of interest to you and expand your knowledge from there based on your needs.

Myth #3: You have to own a large piece of land

The size of land and the ownership of such land is another customizable piece of data in off-the-grid living. Larger pieces of land can give you more options and opportunities, but they can also come with many headaches, like security and maintenance. Self-sustainable living can come from a small piece of land.

You do not have to own land either to live off the grid. You can lease or lend property. Money exchange does not have to be in the cards. Perhaps you may know someone with an unused piece of land. You can offer to care for it in exchange for settling a home there.

Myth #4: It is dangerous

It is sad to say that in the times that we live in, there is no 100% safe place to live. However, no matter where you decide to settle, on or off the grid, you have to mitigate the risks of living in that space. Off-the-grid living means learning to prepare for any possible situation that may occur. Learn to defend yourself, your family, and your home by using the tips provided in this book and others to come. Be proficient in first-aid. Have survival tools on hand, such as candles, batteries, and more. Use a two-way radio or ensure you have a charged phone when you venture away from home. Practice emergency drills with your household, including the kids. The danger level of off-the-grid living is significantly lowered the more prepared you are for possible off-the-wall situations.

Myth #5: You are going to be completely isolated

There are entire communities built off the concepts of off-the-grid living. Examples were stated at the beginning of this book in the form of the Earthships and the Dancing Rabbit EcoVillage. Your level of remoteness from others is a choice.

Despite this misconception, most people who go off the grid, settle close to other people and have neighbors who are within walking distance of them. Where you choose to go off the grid is a matter of how much social interaction you want. Some people want to be isolated with little face-to-face happenings with other people while some love the energy of socializing with other like-minded people.

Myth #6: You can't earn a living

This is also a misconception, especially in the age of the internet. Some people run internet businesses from the comfort of their homes and never see another person during the course. Others have remote jobs. Being a virtual assistant is one such title.

If you prepare the act of earning a living that involves interacting with people in person, you can still set up a business near or in your home. People need entrepreneurs almost everywhere on this planet. You can also work full-time or part-time, depending on the exact location you settle off the grid.

The best thing about off-the-grid living is that you are not tied to any one way of making money to sustain your wants and needs. You can choose to pursue one of these options or even mix and match.

We have debunked many of the popular myths surrounding off-the-grid living and see that most of the rumors are just hot smoke being blown by people who are either misinformed or who misunderstand. While the practice is not for the faint of heart, it is by no means the hard and tough life many crack it up to be.

My best advice is to do some research about people who have made a go at off-the-grid living. What are their experiences like? What are the challenges they discovered and how did they overcome them? How did they transition into that type of living? Answer these and more questions. If you find a success story of someone who lives off the grid in a way that you admire, try to emulate what they did. Know what you want and need out of off-the-grid living and develop a plan to make it happen.

Chapter 2 - The Pros and Cons of Living Off the Grid

One way to determine if off-the-grid living is right for you is to weigh the pros against the cons. This section highlights both sides of the scale for you.

The Pros

Low-Utility Bills

This is the advantage that initially attracts many people to the possibilities that exist with this type of life. At the least, there is little to no expense in the form of electric bills. If you go off the grid with all other utilities, this will apply across the board.

Utility bill payments are an expensive part of living in the modern world. Off-the-grid living allows you to keep that money in your pocket and apply it to things that matter more to you.

You are in Control

Independence and autonomy are the second most common reasons that many choose off-the-grid living. Living on the grid means being reliant on others to supply your basic needs, like utilities. But with off-the-grid living, you take control of these matters and facilitate methods to provide for yourself. You can install systems that give you electricity, running water, heating, cooling, and sewer. Add to that, you will not have to worry about outages or even being held hostage by utility companies and government policies about such things.

It is a Sustainable Way of Living

Utility companies provide largely based on using up our natural resources. There is a growing human population with growing needs. So, they use up these resources at an increasing rate every year. Eventually, they are going to deplete these natural resources. That will spell disaster for us all.

Living off the grid gives us an eco-friendly alternative that leaves a small carbon footprint. That benefits us all.

The Cons

It has a High Initial Cost

There are many advantages to off-the-grid living, but downsides also exist. This is one of the disadvantages that turn many people off the idea. While off-the-grid living is doable in the long-term, there is a good-sized investment that needs to be made upfront. For example, there may be the expense of buying land, building a home, setting up gardens, or setting up systems to provide electricity, heat, running water, etc.

There is Some Grunt Work

While someone else maintains the systems that provide utilities on the grid, taking yourself off the grid means that you have to do this work.

Now that you are armed with the good and bad of what it takes to live off the grid, does the good outweigh the bad or vice versa for you?

Chapter 3 – Preparing for Off-Grid Living

Living off the grid can be difficult. It is not for everyone. However, people who appreciate the benefits of it and prefer to give merit to the reward instead of the possible challenge give it a go. Some go back to the grid but others—a special build of people—love everything about it, even the challenges. Are you one of those people? If you are, this section helps you with the transition period.

The first thing you need to prepare is your mind. Going off the grid is not about isolating yourself in a cabin in the woods. Even if that is the way you decide to go, the true gift is the independence that comes with making such a life change. Even if you still decide to enjoy some of the luxuries that civilization has to offer, you have to understand that independence comes with responsibilities. It comes with planning and preparation. All of those things can be mentally taxing, especially if you were not prepared for the burden.

Therefore, the first thing I would advise you to do is flex your mental muscles. Look at how this lifestyle shift might work out in your mind first.

Things to Consider

To help you create that mental picture, here are a few things that you must consider before you go off the grid:

- Will you need electricity?

    If the answer is no, consider the items that you will use for light, such as candles, lamps, or a fireplace. If yes, how will you generate this? Options will be listed in the coming pages.

- Where is your water source?

    You cannot live without clean water, so sourcing needs to be figured out immediately. It is especially important to have access to drinkable water. Where will you get this?

- Do you want to live in a community setting?

    Just how social do you want to remain? If you are an extrovert, this is a serious consideration. Living off the grid is not meant to make you feel miserable. You can still interact with others regularly as long as you choose the right setting to settle down.

- How much money will you need?

    Remember that initial investment is needed to sustain this way of living. Understanding where you are going, the housing that you will be sheltered by, and all the other details that go into it will allow you to create a financial plan for the initial move and over the long haul.

- How will you get money?

    Will you be a business owner? Will you find employment nearby? Will you be a digital nomad? Will you live off investments? Income is an important part of comfortable living. Have it figured out before you go off the grid. This will allow you to understand the tools you need. For example, a digital nomad or an entrepreneur might need internet access to sustain the way they earn their income. How will you set this up?

- How will you source food?

Will you be buying it or growing it? Perhaps hunting for it? A combination of all or more options?

You might feel overwhelmed looking at the list of considerations above, but I assure you that it is quite doable to tick everything off. Just take things one step at a time. It is better to think things over thoroughly in the beginning rather than feel lost, figuratively and literally, after you have made the shift.

Steps to Take for Off-Grid Living

After considerations have been made, if your heart is still pumping to do this, here are the summarized steps of how to take yourself off the grid:

Read Everything You can About Off-Grid Living

Information and knowledge are your best bet for transitioning into off-the-grid living as seamlessly as possible. So, soak it up. Read articles and blog posts about and from people doing this. Watch videos on preparation resources. Reading books such as this one helps you get down to the nitty-gritty of it. Inform yourself so that you are as prepared as possible beforehand. The best thing is that most of these resources are free. Just make sure you are viewing reliable sources and that you keep in mind that everyone's experiences are slightly different. Even if you are smack-dab in the middle of a city right now, you can know what it means to live off the grid.

Find the Best Location Possible

Location affects your cost of living. There are items like the land availability, property taxes, building codes to be met, landholding opening (leasing, etc.) that affect the living standard you can afford.

You might have an ideal location in mind. Some people choose to live in a location with a climate different from what they are accustomed to. Be mindful that you are used to the cost of that area.

Based on Your Location, Study the Possibilities of Shelter

Your exact dwelling in this location is dependent on that location, if you are being practical, that is. For example, it might not be practical to build a cabin in a tropical location or a bungalow in a low temperature location. We will discuss housing options in the next section.

When you have the type of dwelling nailed down, you need to then make the following considerations:

- How much square footage do you need?
- Will you be building a home or moving into already established housing?
- If you are building, what type of materials work best in that climate? How will you transport this material and how much will it cost?
- How will you finance this? Will you be buying, leasing, or renting?

To help you make as informed a decision about these and other details as possible, visit the area that you plan to settle down in. Note the living conditions in and around it. Pay attention to the building materials used most commonly and other details in the surrounding houses.

Examine Your Energy and Water Options

Next, it is time to examine the electrical power and water options available in that area. This is again dependent on the location that you have chosen. Some locations have renewable energy options that work as stand-alone. Some options whereby your energy consumption cost is reduced to zero. As part of the research of the area, note what is available.

The size of your home affects this, too, as some options work better with different sizes. Options include generators, wind power, battery systems, and solar power. We will discuss these options and more in the next section.

The location also affects your water supply options. You may need to have water delivered to your home if piping is not already installed. Therefore, the well drilling and installation of pumping may be necessary. If there is a nearby body of water that you can source water from, how will this work? Special consideration needs to be paid to drinking water availability and quality, especially if you are relying on a nearby natural water supply, such as a lake. This needs to be filtered and sterilized to make it healthy for consumption.

Water storage in and around your home is a must. Will you be installing tanks to facilitate this?

With both electricity and water considerations, you need to look at the cost, labor, and practicality of each. How you have electricity and water installed into your home needs to be a sustainable practice that does not drill a hole in your pocket unnecessarily.

Figure out Where Your Food Supply will Come From

The next consideration is how you will source your food. Will you be self-reliant and self-sufficient in this environment by hunting, fishing, and trapping food? Will you set up a garden? Will you be making use of local supermarkets and grocery stores? Will you take a hybrid approach? There is no right or wrong answer. Do what works for you. Do not be surprised if these practices change over time as you adapt to your unique circumstances.

If you will be participating in the first practice mentioned, you need to become familiar with the hunting, fishing, and trapping licenses that are necessary in that area. What items are legally obtained in what seasons? Are there any endangered species?

If you are gardening, you need to know which produce and herbs grow best in an area and what practices you need to adopt to get the healthiest and most nutritionally rich end product. How much will you grow if you have a garden? How can you keep this as low maintenance as possible? How will you preserve the food obtained from the garden when you have excess?

There is also the option of foraging for wild plants to gain produce. What are the legalities on this in the area? What are the specific areas that you can practice foraging in? What are the options? How can you sustainably harvest what is available?

Will you also be incorporating livestock on the property? If yes, what type of livestock will you keep and how will you raise them? How will you house them?

If you will be shopping for items, what are the shopping options available to you? How close are they to the dwelling? Will you need transportation to get to them?

Explore Off-Grid Money-Making Options

Sustaining your lifestyle is facilitated by the income that you are earning on or off the grid. Unless your financial future is secured with pension income or you live off investments, you need to find a way to earn an income even when you live off the grid.

Luckily, there are a variety of options, such as online freelancing; selling homemade products; offering services, such as woodworking; selling produce; and even gaining employment nearby.

Network with Others Who are Living off the Grid

As mentioned before, living off the grid does not mean that you have to isolate yourself. In fact, I recommend that you do not, as this is not a healthy mental practice. Living off the grid should be just as enjoyable as living on it and healthy human interaction is part of that equation.

When you are researching locations, note the populations of the areas and how close your neighbors are. Enjoy that you get the amount of social interaction that is comfortable for you.

Chapter 4 – The Details of Off-Grid Living

Let's expand on the finer details of living off the grid by looking at what your options are when it comes to housing, electricity, water, food, and more.

Types of Houses

Shelter is a basic necessity, whether you live on or off the grid. Narrowing down the option can be an intimidating aspect of figuring things out as you move off the grid. The space that you get is dependent on your location, of course, but also on your desires and what you can afford.

Your housing options, which can be adapted to any location, include:

Tiny Houses

If you want to ditch the long-term commitment and cost of the mortgages of your typical home, then getting a tiny home may be for you. The definition of a tiny home is given away in the name, as it is basically a miniaturized house. It is typically no bigger than the living room of your average house. Because the living space is downsized, a minimalistic approach is typically the way to go when it comes to acquiring belongings.

One of the greatest advantages of owning a tiny home is that it can be easily relocated to different plots of land and communities. This allows you to be flexible, as you are not tied to a particular location. You can move this home with you to another.

Small house construction is a big market, and there are quite a few options. They can also be customized to suit your needs.

Shipping Containers

This is a quick and simple solution, as these are already shaped like a house. All you have to do is make a few adjustments, like the addition of windows, to make it into a comfortable living space. Insulation can be added for colder climates and cooling systems can be installed for warmer locations.

Just like tiny homes, shipping containers allow flexibility with location. There is also the possibility of expanding this by connecting or stacking several containers.

RV

If you have not found any one location that is perfect for you, or you like to travel, then getting an RV is the way to go. This is the perfect option for people who do not want to be tied to any specific address.

Advantages of this type of dwelling include not having to pay rent, to buy land, or to pay local taxes. Note that you do have to pay for gas, but this can be minimized.

Just like the other options listed above, a good RV includes a sleeping area, kitchen, toilet, shower, and living room. You can have a home on wheels.

Cabins

This is typically the image that people automatically adopt when they think of off-the-grid living. This is typically a smaller home that is found in a more remote location. While it is possible to build your own cabin, there are options available for purchase. People who invest in cabins tend to live off the land by hunting, fishing, farming, and trapping. Cabins are thought to be the truest form of the off-the-grid experience.

Electricity

While going off the grid does mean that you disconnect from the traditional grid system of gaining electricity, that does not mean you have to do without this type of power. You can generate electricity on your own property. The same applies to gas.

Options for generating your own electricity include:
- Solar panels. Power from the sun is harnessed by these to give you electricity.
- Wind turbines. Also called windmills, these use the power of the wind to generate electricity.
- Geothermal. These systems extract heat from the earth to generate electricity.
- Micro-hydro. The equipment uses the natural flow of water to generate electricity.
- Power Generators. These are not a renewable source of electricity like the others mentioned, but they are a convenient backup to have.
- Natural gas generators. These are a more renewable way to make use of generators, as they generate electricity using natural gas instead of choices like propane, gasoline, or diesel.

Finding Food

When you live off the grid, you need to know how to prepare, grow, and store food. Some of the most readily available and convenient options include easier-to-store items with a long shelf life like:
- Dried food
- Canned food
- Spices, sugars, and salts

We have already gone through preservation methods, like drying and canning. The same methodologies apply just as the storage techniques do. These items are lightweight and also easy to make and to use. Not to mention, they are delicious.

You do not have to give up on fresh food, though. Some of the best choices for fresh food to be consumed living off the grid include:

- Fruits
- Vegetables
- Fish
- Seafood
- Eggs
- Meat

You can, of course, grow your own garden to obtain fruits and vegetables. Some of the lowest maintenance and nutritious options include beans, corn, and berries.

You can obtain fish and seafood from a nearby water source. However, you can grow your own fish off the grid in the practice called fishing culture. Also called aquaculture, you do this by developing the appropriate environment and raising the desired species of fish in that managed space. You can take this up a notch by creating a fish farm. The quantities obtained from this are plenty, so you can sell your gains for profit.

The other options on the list are best found by raising livestock. Eggs can be laid by chickens, but you can also obtain eggs from animals like geese, quail, turkey, pheasant, and ducks. You can raise livestock like rabbits, cows, sheep, and goats for meat. Raising your own livestock means that you also have a source of daily products, like milk, cheese, yogurt, and butter. The best part is that raising animals is relatively inexpensive.

Hunting options can include small game, like beavers and woodchucks.

Finding Water

The first order of business when it comes to ensuring that you have water for drinking, hygiene practices, and more is sourcing it. Typically, water is sourced for off-the-grid living in the following ways:

- Stream
- River
- Dam
- Groundwater
- Rainwater

Once the source is secure, you need to collect this water. The collection is a multiple-level activity that involves the following components:

- Catchment surface, such as a roof for rainwater.

- Conveyance or diversion system to direct the water into the storage system.
- Storage systems, which can be options like water tanks and cisterns. Cisterns allow the storage of large amounts of water. You can do this above ground or below ground. The options below ground offer the bulkier storage options.
- Distribution system, which is the delivery of the stored water to your homes, garden, and wherever else on the property that needs it.
- Treatment system, which is the treatment or filtration of the water to make it safe to consume. This treatment can be done in any of the following ways:
  - DIY biofilters
  - UV/sunlight
  - Ceramic filters
  - Chemical disinfectant
  - Distillation
  - Boiling

Cooking

I would not advise you to use an electric stove or oven while living off the grid, as they can become useless if your electricity supply is cut off. They are also not a high conservation. Instead, the next few options allow you to cook no matter the electricity situation and are greener. They also make great backup solutions if electric stoves and ovens are your preference.

- Camp stoves, which offer an experience similar to cooking on a stovetop. They are, however, portable and smaller.
- Solar dehydrator, which harnesses the power of the sun to cook. Great for creating jerky or salt fish.
- Solar ovens, which work just like regular ovens, but instead they use the sun as the fuel source.
- Fire pits, which use wood as the fuel source.
- Rocket stoves, which also use small pieces of wood as the fuel source.

Book 15 – Waste & Hygiene

Because of the nature of this topic, many people try to skip over it, but doing so will only leave you in a dirty situation ... pun intended. Waste can pile up quickly and, in emergencies, the garbage truck might not be making its scheduled runs and the sewer main may be shut down. Living off the grid means that you take on the responsibility of managing waste yourself, regardless of whether it's a time of emergency or not. You also need to figure out how to keep yourself and your surroundings clean. This section addresses the issues.

The Steps to Managing Waste

Leaving waste unattended around your property will attract insects, animals, and bacteria. That is an unhealthy environment, as it also serves as a breeding ground for disease. Even if you are actively trying to produce less waste, you will produce some quantity. During disasters (natural and manmade) or a pandemic, waste production increases. How do you dispose of this? Here are the steps for doing so:

Start Sorting

This practice is one that you should practice whether you are living through endangered times or not, or whether you live on the grid or not. You need to take an inventory of the waste that you produce. On average, the EPA (U.S. Environmental Protection Agency) estimates that an American household produces the following approximate percentages of household waste:

- Paper and cardboard - 26%
- Yard and food - 28%
- Rubber leather and textiles - 9%
- Metal - 9%
- Wood - 6%
- Glass - 4%

Different types of waste need to be disposed of differently, and this means that the first thing that you need to do is sort it all out. Use different bins to collect different types of waste to make the next steps easier and to prevent cross-contamination if it is applicable.

Composting Food Waste

Try as much as possible to limit the use of packaged food and use as many naturally produced foods, like veggies, fruits, and meat, as possible. Producing less waste includes using leftovers and ensuring that you eat foods before they spoil. Still, some kind of food wastage is always made. For example, the simple act of peeling a potato produces waste in the form of skins. Food wastage quickly attracts insects and animals. Luckily, most food waste can be placed in a compost pile.

Composting is a process of recycling organic matter. It happens naturally in processes such as when leaves fall to the ground. But you can also facilitate this process by turning food scraps into fertilizer to enrich your soil and help your garden grow to its full potential. All you have to do is throw foodstuff into an assigned box, along with green matter, like leaves, and brown matter, like dead plants.

Vermicomposting is also an option. This is the process by which worms are used to facilitate the composting process so that a hummus-like end product, known as vermin-compost, is produced. Composting is a great option if you have a limited amount of space.

If you live in a space, like an apartment building, where square footage is limited, compost can be brought to the nearest green spot, such as a public park.

Living off the grid, if you have the means, all you have to do is find an appropriate location on the property and set up your bin there. The space needs to be well-draining, or you risk creating a hazard. Add brown matter, such as fallen leaves, bush trimmings, and grass clippings to this bin.

Be mindful that there are food waste items that cannot be composted. These include milk, cheese, lard, oil, grease, meat, and bones.

These items attract animals, such as rats, which can spread disease. You do have the option of feeding food scraps, like meat and bones, to family pets instead.

Other items that cannot be added to the compost pile include:
- Human and animal feces, including diapers
- Treated wood
- Diseased plants
- Plants that have been treated with chemicals

Burning Waste

Burning waste is dangerous and is generally not recommended. However, during times of emergency, where the government has collapsed, this is an option to maintain sanitation and good health.

Items that can be burned include cardboard, paper, some types of food, and textiles. If you do indeed decide to burn waste, be mindful of fire safety practices. Burn in small, controllable batches that are removed from plants and buildings. Do not start fires on a lawn. Make a pit to burn the waste in. Keep water nearby in case the fire starts to spread. Never leave a fire unattended.

Burning waste is not only discouraged because of the possible risk of starting a fire but also because the resulting smoke can be poisonous, and there are items that can explode. Therefore, you need to be mindful of the things that you cannot burn. Such items include:

- Paper products with ink on them
- Items that hold chemicals, like fertilizer containers or bleach bottles
- All metals
- Plastic
- Rubber
- Treated wood
- Human and animal feces

While there are industrial incinerators that can handle burning a few of these items, they burn far hotter than is typical for a backyard fire and need a lot of well-ventilated space. The risk is not worth the reward in most cases, by my estimation.

Reduce Waste

Try to reuse as many of the items that you use to reduce the amount of waste that you produce. Paper can be used as toilet paper. Cardboard boxes can be flattened and stacked, stored away for instances when they might come in handy. Leather and textiles can be stored and used to patch torn clothes or to dress wounds. Some plastic containers and bottles may be used to store water. Never use containers or bottles that once held chemicals or non-foodstuff as storage water and other storage items. That also applies to metal and glass containers. Reuse plastic bags as storage containers.

Bury Waste

If an item cannot be composted, burned, or reused, the final option is to bury it. Use a space that will not be used as garden square footage in the future. Mark the spot clearly and dig into it deep enough so that animals cannot dig the waste back up. It is recommended that you have at least a foot and a half above the waste after it has been buried. Items that can be buried include treated wood, rubber, metal, and plastic.

Burying Human Waste

What do you do if you cannot flush the toilet and do not expect sewer service to be available to you? Just like with items that cannot be composted, buried, or reused, you must bury human waste.

As a temporary solution, you can dig a small but deep hole, place your business in there, and then cover the hole.

If you do not have sewer service for more than a few days, a more permanent solution is to build a latrine. A latrine is an outhouse or an outdoor toilet. It is recommended that you build a trench that is at least 4 feet deep and 18 inches wide. Place logs across this hole so that you can sit on them, leaving only enough space for you to use. Cover the latrine with some kind of lid to prevent flies from getting in when it is not being used. Flies cause the growth of bacteria and viruses.

You also have the option of using disinfectants and lime to sanitize the latrine and keep unwanted smells down, but this can also kill the good bacteria that decompose the waste. This can actually cause more unwanted smells and develop an environment where disease is created. Be sure to set up a hand washing station nearby with water and soap.

A few final recommendations for using a latrine safely include limiting its use to your family and wearing shoes when you go out to use it.

General recommendations for burying waste include:
- Using an area that is at least 200 feet away from your water source.
- Do not use an area where water collects.
- Label the area for that particular use.
- After the area has been used completely, cover with at least a foot and a half of dirt. If the area sinks, add more dirt.

Staying Clean off the Grid

Modern toilets, showers, and even bathtubs need not be a sacrifice if you live off the grid. However, to maintain cleanliness, even during an emergency, you should also explore other options for keeping clean.

Always keep water conservation in your mind in your personal hygiene practices. For example, if you have created an outdoor shower, it is a good idea to install a stand-in water collecting device, such as a tub or a wading pool, to catch the used water. This can be used to facilitate practices such as watering plants or flushing toilets.

Other ways that you can maintain personal hygiene off the grid include using a traveling shower. These are portable showers that you can carry around and get clean whenever you want wherever you want. This is a one-time purchase that you can carry with you, and the best part is that you can have a warm shower by letting the refillable water bags sit in the sun for a few hours.

The use of wipes and waterless body showers and shampoos are also an option. They foam up as you would expect but do not need to be rinsed. They are a great means of conserving water while keeping clean.

The next part in this book series will go over some lifestyle prepping and how you can live as long as possible with disastrous scenarios and how to prepare for them.

Book 16:

The Lifestyle: Surviving as Long as Possible

Imagine surviving adrift at sea all alone in a small boat for more than a year. Seems like the stuff of fiction, doesn't it? Surviving 1 week seems like an impossibility, yet a man called José Salvador Alvarenga spent 13 months drifting on the high seas and survived to tell the tale. The Salvadoran fisherman is the first person in recorded history to have survived for more than a year under such circumstances. Let's take a look at his story.

It was November 17, 2012, and José set out with fellow fisherman, Ezequiel Cordoba, from a fishing village on Mexico's southern border into the Pacific Ocean. Their task was to hunt tuna, shark, and mahi mahi for about 30 hours and then return. Unfortunately, a storm blew in just a few hours into the trip, and the 2 men were blown off course. The storm lasted 5 days, and the boat's motor was damaged in the process.

The men called for help on the boat's radio before it was disabled. A search party was sent to rescue the men, but it was abandoned after 2 days with the assumption that the men had drowned when no sign of them was found.

The two men were on their own. Without food or fresh water, the men resorted to eating raw fish, jellyfish, and turtles. They drank turtle blood and rainwater. 4 months in, Ezequiel died after becoming ill.

José was on his own.

Another 9 months went by. It seemed hopeless until José spotted a small island. He had reached the Marshall Islands. He jumped off his boat and swam to shore where he met a local couple. They called in the authorities. The man everyone had thought dead was indeed alive.

While we would like to believe that he survived off sheer will and determination alone, they were only part and parcel of what ensured he made it.

God forbid that something of that magnitude happens to you, but you need to think in those terms to be prepared to survive. This section puts you into these imaginary situations and shows you just how you can make it out alive like José did.

Chapter 1 – The Beginning of Your Preparation

We rely heavily on the social constructs that we have developed in the modern world, but that structure will collapse at the first sign of impending doom. While zombie apocalypses can seem far-fetched, many scenarios are easier to imagine and more likely to occur. These are called SHTF scenarios. Knowing, understanding, and preparing for them can mean the difference between you living through them or not.

The SHTF Scenarios

SHTF is an acronym for "Shit Hits The Fan." It is meant to signify any arising situation where there is a breakdown of the modern world as we know it. Hurricane Katrina signifies an SHTF event, but so does the civil unrest that a war might cause or a cyberattack where user information is compromised or stolen. During such times, it is okay to assume that you cannot rely on conventional means of aid, like the police department, fire department, or even the government. You have to be self-sufficient enough to make it on your own.

The exact preparation for an SHTF event is dependent on the exact type of event. The types of SHTF events that you likely need to be prepared for include:

Natural Disasters

Examples of such disasters include hurricanes, tornadoes, wildfires, floods, tsunamis, earthquakes, or any other intense natural event that causes damage to infrastructure and human life. The more intense this natural disaster, the more likely you will be on your own afterward.

World War

There is a lot of unrest and conflict on a global scale in the modern age, and even though it is approaching a century since the last world war, things can explode literally and figuratively at any time. There is no way of knowing how close you would be to the battlefield and, thus, the destruction and carnage. Therefore, preparing for a world war is slightly different from preparing for a natural disaster since we tend to know which ones are most likely in our area.

Grid Down

There are many reasons why the power grid might fail, including natural disasters or simply failing due to old age. Panic will set in, in such an event, creating many unsafe circumstances.

Food Crisis

Food supply can be interrupted for many reasons, including a disaster or a pandemic. You need to not only prepare by ensuring that your pantry is well stocked, but you also must be prepared to protect yourself from persons who are hungry and likely dangerous.

Global Warming

Climate change and rising temperatures around the globe lead to bigger natural disasters and rising sea levels, which can cause secondary disasters, like food shortages and downed power grids.

Economic Collapse

Recessions and economic depression are a part of economic life on this planet. No matter how well the economy is performing, always be prepared for such circumstances as buying food supplies and getting the essentials for living becoming more difficult.

Pandemic

The outbreak of Covid-19 shows how fragile our economic systems are and how susceptible they are to deadly diseases and viruses. Life is even more fragile.

There is no one size fits all SHTF scenario as things develop on the ground at the time, but you can learn to have a general preparedness plan for each scenario.

Preparing for the Worst

So, how do you prepare for the unthinkable? Here are a few tips for doing just that:

Practice Using Less Electricity

We live in a time when we are dependent on electricity to do almost everything. From charging our phones to cooking and even helping us fall asleep. However, when shit hits the fan, that is usually the first utility that is taken from us. Using less electricity now is the only way that you can note how you would survive during a situation where the grid is shut down. There are several ways in which you can use electricity less. Ideas include:

- Using freezers less to store food and relying more on bulk food and freeze-dried food.
- Store and use more batteries for items like radios.

- Use wind-up devices. There is a long list of such energy-saving devices, like cell phone chargers and flashlights.
- Have a backup electricity supply, such as a generator.

Maintain a Survival Notebook

We look at the internet to educate ourselves and keep informed. This includes maintaining preparedness and survival information during disasters. But if the electricity goes down, more than likely, internet access will, too. There may even be instances where websites that aid in your survival may be blocked even if you could access the internet.

Prepare for such an instance by accumulating preparedness notes in a survival notebook. You can enhance this by getting a few books to develop a survival library.

Make Learning a Habit

Being self-sufficient means that you need to be a Jack of all trades. Taking on such a mindset means that you embrace that you need to learn new skills and become more proficient at those that you already have. Look into skills that would be handy in the SHTF events that are likely to occur in your area and make it a point to learn as many of these as you can. Start with those skills that you enjoy most so that you are not put off the task.

Learning also means reading, watching videos, taking courses, and other mental nourishing activities that add to the mental banking you are keeping to help you survive the worst. Take notes about important facts and handy procedures in your survival notebook.

Learning will be even more enjoyable, and you will be accountable if you get a learning buddy.

Practice Growing Your Own Food

This practice will get you less dependent on the typical food supply. While you may not be able to grow all the food that you need, you can keep a garden that will supply at least a portion. Even if you live in a tiny apartment, you can create a garden, such as a container garden or a vertical garden. All you have to do is get creative with your space.

Prepare Yourself for Fear and Panic

Fear and panic are an inevitable part of experiencing a disaster of any kind. That is, after all, why you prepare for disasters beforehand. These are normal human emotions in the face of stressful times. Acknowledge what you feel and do what it takes to move on during these hard times

Extra Preparedness Steps

You can go above and beyond by implementing a few more steps to your preparing-for-the-worst plan. Such measures include:

Identifying the threats

Far too often, we adopt a mindset thinking that disasters and other ill events cannot happen to us, but the truth is that anything can happen to anyone at any time. The worst-case scenario can become your reality on any given day of the week, so it is best to prepare for it to manage the fallout.

While you have no way of knowing exactly what will happen, some disasters are more likely to happen compared to others in certain locations and under certain conditions. For example, people who live in California along the San Andreas fault line should be more prepared for earthquakes compared to people who live in New York. People who live on the US East Coast should be more prepared for hurricanes compared to people who live on the western borders. People who live in the Midwest should have tornado preparedness locked down and not focus on tsunamis.

Knowing what is most likely to happen in that particular area allows you to learn about the occurrences that are typical during such events. When you know what to expect, you can better develop an appropriate preparedness plan.

Mental Preparedness

Your mental health has a huge impact on the successful preparation and implementation of a preparedness plan. It will not matter how much food you stock or if you have the best laid out garden if you make bad decisions at the times that it matters most to keep a cool head.

Condition your mind to acknowledge and accept what is going on then go into overdrive during emergencies. Develop the mental muscle for doing this with mental drills, just as you would train your body with exercise repetitions. Imagine the bad scenarios in detail. If tornadoes are likely to happen in your location, imagine the sound of the tornado warning going off. Imagine seeing the whirling mass of wind touching down on the ground. Imagine feeling the wind pull at your clothes and roar in your ears. Also imagine yourself going into action to survive. Imagine it all and trick your brain into thinking you have already been through this. Make it so that your brain responds automatically in case this does become reality. Otherwise, you risk freezing up and not taking the action you have planned out.

Assessing your preparedness

A good disaster preparedness plan is contingent on you noting your current level of preparedness. This means going through the supplies in your home, noting your current level of defense, understanding how your household responds to injuries and sickness, noting your current level of dependency on the grid and more.

Once that assessment has been done and recorded, you can build on your strength and focus on tightening up your weak spots. Make a list of all the items you need to source to be prepared.

Creating a budget for your prepping

Once your assessment is prepared, you can then create a costing of what you need to get on par with the level of preparedness you need. Create a budget from this. Do not rush out and buy everything at one time, especially not all the fancy gears and gadgets that some would have you believe is necessary for survival. Decide how much money you can or want to invest in prepping then focus on priority items on your list.

The Emergency Hygiene Kit

Sanitation and cleanliness are an often overlooked part of disaster preparedness. It shouldn't be, as being unclean can lead to contracting illnesses and getting infections. Additionally, being clean and looking good allows you to feel better mentally. This helps you take on a more positive outlook so that you can gather your determination to get through the hard times.

Luckily, you will not fall into such an unprepared category with the following emergency hygiene kit items stocked and ready to be used:

- Soap
- Toothpaste
- Toothbrush
- Razor
- Dental floss
- Deodorant
- Shampoo
- Conditioner
- Sun shower
- Baking soda (an alternative to shampoo or toothpaste)
- Laundry soap
- Potty bucket
- Kitty litter
- Toilet paper

- Paper towels
- Mobile washer
- Microfiber cloths
- Sanitizer

Chapter 2 – The Scenarios

You never know what life will throw at you, especially in times of disaster and mayhem. However, you can implement the following general steps that should help prepare you no matter the specifics of the trying event:

The General Preparation Steps

Understand Your Threat

We will discuss how to prepare for specific SHTF events soon, but no matter what event occurs, the first step is to educate yourself. You need to determine the chances of the event happening in the area. If it does occur, what would the fallout be? Based on the chances you have determined, when is the next event likely to occur?

Identify the Risks

Once the threats have been identified, determine the risks. In what ways are you vulnerable? If this event happens, how will it affect you? Are the dangers directly related to you or are they secondary consequences?

Respond Quickly and Appropriately

You know the threats and the risks. Now you can appropriate your responses. How well you respond is directly related to how well you calculated the threats and risks. Remember that your response needs to account for both the short-term and the long-term. Prioritize short-term planning then move on to the long term. Determine who you can rely on for help if necessary and how you will get informed as the event unfolds.

Sustain Your Survival Necessities

After an SHTF event, going back to the status quo could take a long time, if it ever does make that shift. You cannot rely on outside intervention to care for you and your loved ones. The responsibility is on you. That responsibility includes providing the necessities such as food, water, clothing, shelter, and security, to name a few. Determine how you will be self-sufficient in these ways.

Now that we understand the terms of general preparedness, let's move on to how to react to specific SHTF events.

Scenario #1: Natural Disasters

The first type of SHTF event that we will look at are natural disasters. Natural disasters include hurricanes, tornadoes, tsunamis, floods, and more. A plan of preparedness for natural disasters includes the following steps:

Make a Plan

Such a plan includes noting emergency phone numbers and keeping them in an easily accessible place, such as on your refrigerator and programmed into your cell phone. You also need to have an emergency supply kit prepared. Ensure that you know the nearest shelters and different routes of evacuation.

Pet owners need to also ensure that their pets are cared for by noting pre-identified shelters and pet-friendly hotels that accept animal stays. You can also get in contact with a friend or family member who will take your pets in the event of an evacuation.

Gather Your Supplies

Ensure that you have all the supplies necessary for your emergency kit, as you may be cut off from the normal supplies of food, water, utilities, and healthcare in the aftermath of a natural disaster. Items that should be included in this kit include:

- Food
- Water
- Medical supplies
- Emergency power sources, like flashlights and extra batteries
- Important documents, such as passports, wills, and personal identification

Know the Difference Between "Watch" and "Warning"

Ensure that you understand the different advisories being televised and announced on radios and online. There are two different kinds of alerts. The first is known as a watch, which means that a natural disaster will *possibly* occur in the stated areas. The other advisory is a warning. This announces that the natural disaster is *expected* to occur in the stated area.

Get Your Family Ready

Go over your emergency plan with your family and be sure to check for regular updates on the natural disaster from a reliable source. If you have a family member who is disabled, be sure to call the public health department or a hospital to cater to their special needs. Put farm animals and pets in a safe place during natural disaster situations.

Prepare Your Home

Prepare your home as best as it can withstand the conditions of the natural disaster. Actions that you can take to do so include:

- Covering up doors and windows with storm shutters such as in areas prone to hurricanes
- Keep your yard clean so that there is no flying debris.
- Ensure that you can safely turn off your power in events such as flooding, downed power lines or if you have to leave your home quickly
- Ensure that clean water containers are filled with drinking water
- Prevent carbon monoxide poisoning by checking your detector's battery

Be Prepared for an Evacuation at any Moment

Listen to the authorities and be ready to move to safety if that is advised. The steps to safely evacuating your home include:

- Grab your emergency supply kit with only the things that you need, such as medicines, cell phones, charges, personal identification, and cash.
- Unplug your appliances and, if there is time to do so, also the gas, water, and electricity
- Follow emergency workers' instructions on the road if there is traffic. Do not drive through flooded areas, as vehicles can easily be swept away or become stuck.

Scenario #2: War

While we might not want to think about the conflict that arises on such a tremendous scale, it is best to be prepared for the unthinkable. The steps to prepare for a war include:

Sign Up for Emergency Alerts

This includes signing up for the alerts of security procedures, knowing how your community will be alerted and signing up for alerts or apps on your cell phone.

Create a Family Emergency Plan

Take a page out of preparing for a natural disaster, and you will be prepared in this area, as well.

Prepare a Disaster Kit

Just like with the emergency kit necessary for preparing for a natural disaster, be sure to have a kit that includes emergency food and water supply, as well as a medicine supply, your important documents, and cash. The fallout of a war may mean that at certain times you will have to move quickly, and you do not want to spend time trying to gather these items then.

Connect with Any Missing Loved Ones

War can quickly divide us, and that means possible separation from your family members and loved ones. Familiarize yourself with programs that help you connect with family members and other loved ones after a war. Such programs include the Federal Emergency Management Agency's National Emergency Family Registry and Locator System and the American Red Cross Safe and Well program. Both of these, and others, allow you to register individuals as safe and to search for persons who have listed themselves as out of danger.

Scenario #3: Global Warming

Even with drastic measures being implemented now to reduce carbon emissions, there is no denying that we have done irreversible damage to the planet. Global warming is a consequence of that and, as such, we are left to deal with terrible outcomes in the form of extreme weather. Some of the main weather events that we are noting in recent history are droughts, heatwaves, and floods. This section addresses how best to prepare for these severe events.

Flooding

A lot of people have the misconception that you need to live near a body of water, like a river, to deal with the risk of flooding. However, once it rains heavily and the water has nowhere to go due to blocked drainage, flooding becomes a problem. This is true even if you live at the top of a hill.

Tips for preparing for a flood include:
- Flood proof your property in the following ways if it is within your means:
    - Build your home on stilts or piers.
    - Install foundation vents or sump pumps.
    - Apply coatings and sealants on your foundations, walls, doorways, and windows to prevent water from coming into your home through cracks.
    - Rase electrical items, like switches, circuit breakers, sockets, and outlets.
    - Point your downspouts away from your home so that the water does not pool around the property.

- Keep valuables, like important documents, on higher ground to prevent possible damage.
- Make sure you have insurance to cover any loss or damage that occurs in case of a flood.
- Avoid tarmac and paving over the garden to prevent water from pooling on the property.

Heatwaves and Drought

Temperatures are rising globally, and that means higher chances of heatwaves and droughts occurring. Things you can do in the short term to protect your home include installing blinds and creating an area of shade to keep cool while outdoors.

The availability of water is an issue under these conditions. Try to conserve water by:
- Using washers and dishwashers only when you have full loads.
- Fixing leaky faucets and turning off taps fully.
- Taking short showers.
- Reusing bath water to water plants.
- Collecting rainwater to water plants and wash your vehicle.
- Using mulch, grass clippings, gravel, or chipped bark as a protective layer in your garden to prevent the loss of moisture.

Scenario #4: Economic Collapse

The Covid-19 pandemic highlighted just how fragile the US economy—one of the strongest economies on the planet—is to SHTF events. This created another SHTF event in the form of an economic recession that has seen high inflation rates, the downturn of many investments, high unemployment rates, pay cuts, and dips in consumer confidence. While the US economy is rebounding nicely in the wake of that pandemic, many other circumstances can cause the economy to collapse, and it can get even worse.

As harsh as this reality is, you can protect your wallet by taking the following actions:
- Pay down your debt so that you have as few monthly payments to make. One of the most costly monthly payments is high-interest debt payments, such as credit card payments. You could be making hundreds of dollars in payments (and potentially more) every month. That is a tight financial squeeze in times when funds are not flowing readily. Keep those funds in your pocket for harsher financial times by eliminating those payments.
- Boost your emergency savings. Try to have at least 6 months' worth of funds to meet your monthly obligations set aside.
- Identify ways to cut back. Keep more money in your pocket by trying to spend less than 30% of your net income on non-compulsory items.
- Live within your means. Do not spend more than you can afford.

- Focus on the long haul. Build a financial portfolio that ensures that you are secure even in the long term. Try to include investments and multiple streams of income in that portfolio.
- Identify your risk tolerance. Assess just how ready you are to withstand an economic downturn. Is your home at risk of being taken by the bank? Are your investments safe even in bad economic situations? What will you do if you lose your main source of income? Do you have backup streams of income that can readily replace that mainstream? Look for the weaknesses in your financial foothold so that you can eliminate them.
- Continue your education and build up skills. Diversify the ways that you can bring in income and invest by educating yourself.

Scenario #5: Pandemic

Dealing with disease and virus outbreaks is not for the faint of heart. But as frightening as it is to endure, you must not panic, even when you are faced with high infection fatality rates. Preparation helps you keep your cool. Ways that you can prepare for a pandemic include:

- Making a plan, such as in other SHTF events.
- Prepare for disruption of services, as supply chains will be affected. There may be other consequences, like economic recessions, employment concerns, and the need to homeschool children.
- Stock up on necessary supplies, like food and water.
- Have access to medical records on both soft and hard copies.
- Ensure your prescriptions are topped up.
- Check your first-aid kit to ensure it is fully equipped.
- Stock up on cleaning supplies to ensure proper hygiene.
- Get vaccinated against the illness, if it is publicly available.

Book 17 – Bugging In and Bugging Out

During an SHTF event, you have two options: either you hold out in your home (bug in) or leave your home to increase your chances of survival (bug out). Let's look at each of these terms in turn.

Many people focus on leaving their home in a time of emergency, but staying bunked in just might be the safer option. This focus stems from the fact that they believe that they have a choice. Often, though, whether you stay bugged in or have to bug out is simply a matter of the particular circumstance. They need to be prepared to do both and either. You are not prepared for an SHTF, even if you cannot handle one or the other. This section shows you how to be prepared no matter what.

Chapter 1 - Bugging in

What is Bugging In?

To be more precise, bugging in is the all-encompassing term that highlights that you plan to stay in your current residence, no matter where it is, to endure the SHTF event. To be clear, bugging in should be the default choice to stay through an emergency. Bugging out should only enter the equation if the risks of staying in outweigh the risks of leaving.

You have the home court advantage in your home during an emergency because you have the legal right to be there. Additionally, all your stuff is there, both your everyday items and your emergency supplies. It is not possible to carry all of these with you when you are out on the road.

You know the ins and outs of your home and your neighborhood. If you need to escape or hide, you know the best routes, and you can improvise on the fly if things go awry. You might even find yourself in a situation where residents of an area are given priority when vaccinations, evacuations, and more occur. You do not want to be the strange one out in these situations.

All in all, bugging in leaves you with fewer unknowns, thus making surviving easier.

Why You Should Choose the Bug-In Strategy

There are many reasons why bugging in might be the best option for you and your household. The first reason is that you might feel safest at home. This is after all, your fort in many ways. Of course, you might have to leave your home if a natural disaster is looming or if personal safety becomes a concern during looting. In such cases, bugging out is the better option. However, if you are adequately prepared for an SHTF event, your home might be the safest place for you and your family and loved ones, as you are stocked with all the things you need and your defenses are in place. If there is no practical reason to leave those comforts, carrying on the minimal, then you should hold down the fort.

The second reason why you might choose to bug in is to ensure the safety of household members who cannot travel. This can include persons who are disabled, pregnant women, and small children.

Additionally, your surroundings at home are familiar to you and the rest of the household. If you leave, you have no idea what you will face. Extreme SHTF events can cut you off from the rest of the world, and if you have no idea what is going on out there, leaving your home might be the bigger risk.

Your exact location can also be an asset in bugging in. People who live in remote areas, like the countryside or in the mountains, tend to have an advantage as long as they are adequately stocked up with food, water, weapons, and more. Such areas are away from starving crowds and civil unrest situations where there might be looting. Additionally, persons in these remote locations tend to be more prepared for the unforeseen compared to people who live in crowded, urban settings.

Leaving your home makes you a stranger to the environment. When you bug in, you are around people within your community. They know you even if you might not be on the friendliest of terms. You are less of a threat to them compared to someone they do not know, and they are less of a threat to you compared to other people you do not know. There is less hostility and less danger. You also have people who are more likely to extend a helping hand to you if it is needed.

Finally, if people from your household or other loved ones have not yet made it to safety, they know exactly where to find you. Bugging out makes locating everyone more difficult.

How to Effectively Bug In

Bugging in is the favored option of the two since the environment is familiar and you can control the conditions there. Still, there needs to be adequate preparation to make this a sound solution in an SHTF event. Planning revolves around how long you can stay in while ensuring everyone in the household is protected. The government recommends keeping supplies on hand to last for at least 3 days for each household member but, as advised before in this book, you need to make considerations for much longer.

At least 2 weeks' worth of supplies must be at the ready to start, but try to achieve at least 6 months' and then 1 years' worth of supply. Remember that utilities may be taken away, and you also have to defend your home. All the previous books in this series will help you bug out, so do revisit any section that you need to. Be prepared to bug out for the long haul.

Even if you have your bugging in plan locked down, you still need to consider that bugging in might not be the safe option. You might have to leave your fortress. You need to have a backup bugging out plan in place, as well.

Chapter 2 - Bugging Out

What is Bugging Out?

Bugging out is the opposite of bugging in. Bugging out is about finding a location apart from your home so that you can set up and tough it through a disaster. Comparing bugging out to bugging in, bugging in seems like the more favorable scenario as long as you are stocked up. You can indeed survive a long time at home as long you have the supplies that you need. As a result, more knowledgeable preppers tend to be more prepared to bug in than to bug out.

Bugging out, in addition to needing more physical endurance, also requires more skill and effort. It also requires some ingenuity as the scenarios that you will face are more unpredictable. However, you cannot count on being able to bug in. You need to consider that you may be forced to bug out. Therefore, you need to be prepared to do just that.

Why You Should Choose the Bug-Out Strategy

So, when should you bug out? Here are circumstances where it tops bugging in:

- When you know that an acute disaster, like a Category 5 hurricane, will make landfall in your area or a planned terrorist attack will be carried out at a certain time in your area.
- If your home becomes a physical threat, such as if the foundations were cracked by an earthquake.
- If there is a dangerous party in your household who is targeting you and making you feel unsafe in that location. An example of this is a domestic violence situation.
- If civil unrest occurs within a block of where you live and those people are being violent.
- If you have exhausted your at-home supplies and scouting the surrounding area does not yield good results.
- If a disaster happens while you are away from your home and getting to that location is dangerous.
- If there is an official government broadcast stating the need to leave the area.

How to Effectively Bug Out

Bugging out safely depends on having a good evacuation strategy. Your plan must be devised around the following factors:

- The SHTF events that are likely to occur around your area. For example, if your area is prone to flood, your bugging out plan will include knowing areas that you can go to that are at higher elevations. Knowing the chances of a disaster occurring in your area allows you to know which evacuation options work in your favor and which should be eliminated from your plan.
- Your strengths and weaknesses. Knowing these allows you to play on your strengths and to mitigate your weaknesses. For example, you might realize that you are fit; therefore, you are better able to carry

heavy and pack more emergency bags. On the other hand, you might realize that you are not knowledgeable about your neighborhood's terrain. You can then plan to go on more hikes to lessen that weakness. Remember the more you educate yourself, thus implementing the things you learn, the more ready to face challenges.

- The possible destinations that you can head to if you have to evacuate. Do not put all your eggs in one basket. Have at least 4 destinations that you can head to in the event that you need to leave your home. Plan these bug-out locations according to the 4 cardinal directions on a map: north, south, west, and east. Pick these locations based on the terrain as well as the chances of the highest risk SHTF events in that area. The more places you can move to, the more flexibility you give yourself when disasters throw their hardest at you. Options for bug-out locations include a second home, a designated camp, a relative's home, a designated shelter and large public facilities. Sometimes, plans do not go as designed. In such cases, seek out parks, forests, factories, campgrounds, and ghost towns as temporary bug-out locations.
- Calculate by what means you will get to these bug-out locations and how quickly you will get to them. This allows you to plan how much you can carry in your emergency kit. Factors that affect how you get to the bug out locations include:
    - The weight of your emergency kit.
    - Your overall level of fitness.
    - The type of geography you are crossing.
    - How many people you will be traveling with and their level of fitness.

If you are getting to these locations on foot, be sure that you plan to hydrate, fuel, and give yourself rest breaks. Also, pack a laminated or waterproof map of your area and those surrounding it so that you can note escape routes and destinations easily. Yes, the map on your phone can be used, but you need to account for situations where the device might not be available to you, such as if it gets lost or the screen gets damaged.

Relating to other people, keep a list of emergency numbers for friends, family, and other loved ones in your emergency notebook. Again, do not rely on the availability of your cell phone. This will help you keep in touch if you get separated from them. Also, keep numbers for government and emergency authorities in there.

If you get separated from your family members, it is good to have a rallying point to get reconnected. This will save time and resources instead of blindly searching for each other. It also means that everyone can get to a safer location fast and with less worry.

Another important part of preparing to bug out is to periodically review your bug-out plan to ensure it remains relevant to your circumstances.

In the next and final book in this series, you will learn exactly what some of the life-saving strategies there are that can really turn the tides of a disaster in your favor.

Book 18:

The Lifestyle: Life-Saving Strategies

When you are faced with a life or death situation, there is no time to act timidly. For better or for worse, you need to bravely and confidently take control of the situation before it controls you.

Laronda Marshall is an example of one such person who has done so. In fact, she has repeatedly proven her mantle.

The Miami bus driver was driving the 40-foot, 15-ton transit bus on a scorcher of a day through the Southern Florida traffic when she was informed that a passenger was slumped over in the back and seemed sick. 50 years old at the time, Laronda swiftly went into action. She parked the bus and went to the back to assess the situation. The man who looked to be in his mid-30s was unconscious and not responsive. The man had no pulse. The situation was dire indeed and cause for many people to panic. But not Laronda. She kept a cool head. In fact, she describes herself as someone who can "stay cool in a crisis." Her ability certainly came in handy on that day.

Laronda was a former nurse's aide, so she was equipped to handle the medical emergency until help arrived. She told another passenger to call 911 while she got to work performing CPR on the man. She continued to do so until the man responded. Emergency personnel arrived about 10 minutes later but, by then, Laronda had gotten the man to breathe again.

On September 19, 2019, Laronda saved the life of a man whom she did not even know. But he was not the first life that the woman had saved. He was the third person in 2 years that this bus driver had saved on her bus route.

The first time that Laronda stepped in to help was also in September, but this time in 2017. She saw a man, who regularly rode the bus, lying in the middle of the road. Apparently, the man, who had been in his 70s at the time, had been hit by a car while he was crossing the road. His leg had been broken because of the incident. He was clearly in need of help, but no one stopped to assist him. Other motorists were just driving by. That is until Laronda rode in on the transit bus. She parked close to the scene and went to comfort the injured man until emergency personnel got there.

Only a month later, she noticed a girl wandering into traffic one morning. The 8-year-old girl had been clutching a Teddy bear and did not speak. The little girl had wandered away from home. Laronda came to the child's aid by getting her on the bus and calling the police, who tracked her parents down.

A cool head can mean the difference between life and death. If Laronda had not kept a cool head, that little girl might have been hit by a vehicle as she walked into traffic, the elderly man might have been even more traumatized by being hit by a vehicle, and the man in the back on her bus might have lost his life. Not only that, her life-saving skills came in handy to get air back into his lungs as she gave his heart the little help it needed to keep on beating.

Laronda is not the only one who showed life-saving abilities in recent times. Matt Uber used CPR to save his young daughter on April 25, 2021. That might not even be the most astounding part. Matt learned the skill from watching the TV show called *The Office*.

Matt and his daughter, Vera, had been playing tag when Matt recalled hearing a thud. He looked over at his daughter to find her curled up into a ball in the corner. He had originally thought that she had tripped, fallen, and hit her head, but when he checked on her, he found her limp with her eyes rolled back. He ordered his older daughter to call 911, but he knew that he could not wait for the help to arrive since the little girl was not breathing and was getting paler by the second.

He channeled the popular character on the show called Michael Scott so that he could do the chest compressions and breaths that he had seen the man do in an episode. The man recalled the reenactment of the life-saving skills, and it meant that his daughter lived. He lifted her neck and made sure that she was not having a seizure or choking.

He said, "It's just what kicks in, what's in your head, and that's fortunate."

What kicked in ensured that his daughter was stable enough to respond to CPR by the time paramedics got to the scene. The little girl had gone into cardiac arrest because of a rare condition called calmodulinopathy. It was only after that incident that the girl was tested and then diagnosed with the life-threatening illness. Treatment led to Vera living and causing mischief, just like any other child her age.

Laronda and Matt are two astounding people. They both thought their way through panic-inducing situations so that they could administer the help that someone else needed. They saved lives by keeping a cool head.

It is important that you not only learn to rationalize your way out of disaster but to also act on life-saving skills. This book in this series teaches you the tools you need to save your life and others. Knowing that you have those skills to depend on certainly goes a long way in helping you think then act when disaster strikes.

The Importance of Life-Saving Skills

You don't have to drive a bus for a living, or even have kids of your own, to learn life-saving skills. In fact, there are a variety of reasons why you should gather such skills under your belt. Such reasons include:

Earns You Mileage in Life

Your career. Participating in hobbies. Going on trips. All of these and other situations where having life-saving skills can come in handy and give you a leg up over people who do not possess the same abilities. You get more opportunities, as other people see you as more competent. You being able to perform CPR or the Heimlich Maneuver can be the reason that you are hired over someone else by a company. It could be the reason why you are called to supervise your kid's road trip over another parent. You will be seen as a potential hero in times of emergency and that makes you automatically more useful.

Easy to Learn

Life-saving skills, like CPR and the Heimlich Maneuver, are not hard to learn. Just like with all other learned abilities, it also looks difficult until you get your footing. No matter your physical or mental limitations or capabilities, you can learn to save a life.

Helps get You Away from Disasters

Typically, when a person learns life-saving skills, these are learned in tandem with other skills that can help you and other people be safer during a disaster.

Prevents Suffering and Helps You Heal Faster

Using life-saving practices can lessen the impact of injuries, make wounds less extensive, and lessen damage done. Therefore, recovery is sped up and suffering is reduced.

Places You in a Position to Possibly Save a Life

Just like Laronda or Matt, you could be the reason why someone lives. You can even save your own life, even if it is to call out instructions on how someone else can impart these skills. Knowing for sure how to perform these maneuvers gives you the confidence to act. On the other hand, if you do not know what to do, you will be uncertain and likely to do the wrong thing. This can leave you vulnerable to lawsuits if things go wrong. It is also heartbreaking to have to stand by while someone else needs help and know that there is nothing that you can do.

Helps Boost Self-Worth

Having the ability to help someone else makes a difference in someone else's life and does wonders to increase confidence and a person's sense of self-worth. On the other hand, feeling helpless during an emergency and not being able to help one's self or others when needed can have the opposite effect. Additionally, feeling helpless can induce panic and cause you to lose your cool.

Invaluable Knowledge

As I have been saying throughout this book, the value of increased knowledge is immeasurable. Learning these skills is useful in all aspects of your life, as you improve the quality of your life and that of other people. You can give other people the same value by teaching them what you have learned.

Offers the Ability to Prevent Health Emergencies

Knowing how to use life-saving skills can be the reason why other dangerous situations do not occur. For example, preventing someone from choking by using the Heimlich Maneuver can mean they walk out of a hazardous situation instead of having to be carried out. This significantly reduces the danger to everyone involved by potentially preventing another disaster from occurring.

Book 19 – Specific Skills to Learn for Disasters

Chapter 1 - Finding Shelter

If you are forced out of your home or need to bug out for any reason, you may find that you need to seek shelter. Unfortunately, these might not be the most comfortable circumstances with the luxuries that we are used to, but you will need to keep as warm as possible and protect yourself from the elements. Options to take such shelter in the wilderness include:

Tree and Bushes

These should not be the main part of your SHTF event survival plan for three reasons:

- They are not suitable for long-term survival, as you are exposed to the elements and other dangers.
- They are not comfortable.
- They are not sustainable. After all, a strong gust of wind can blow the leaves off the tree or bush, or even dismantle it from its locations completely.

However, in the immediate short-term, tree and bush shelters can be the thing that keeps you alive. This is a measure that you take when there is no time to construct a proper shelter. Look for spruce trees, as they have a nearly impenetrable canopy that will keep you dry if it rains. They also have a sturdy trunk for hanging onto if need be. These trunks also serve as a windbreaker. There is normally a thick bed of needles on the ground beneath. They provide a makeshift bed. If there are no spruce trees in the area, simply look for a good alternative with a thick canopy and a sturdy trunk. (NOTE: trees attract lightning, never shelter under or near trees in an electrical storm)

Do not take shelter under trees that are leaning heavily to one side. The same goes for trees that have roots coming out of the ground. If the branches of the tree are too low to provide comfortable space underneath, break off a few to make the space usable.

If you are in greater danger, you can slide underneath bushes. Just be sure that a wild animal did not have the same idea as you and is not already occupying the space. It is actually better if the available space is small in colder conditions, as this allows you to pile debris like leaves around you to act as insulation.

Hollowed Logs

Just like trees and bushes, hollowed logs should not be your go-to option for shelter, but they will do in a pinch. Since they are already raised above the ground and have a cover, they suit the purpose.

To make use of this as a shelter, you first need to locate a downed tree that has a trunk that has started rotting out from the inside out. The center of such a log will be fragile. It may even be partially hollow. Do not try to clean out a tree that is not sufficiently decayed, as this is not worth the effort.

Use a trowel or a hand ax to carve away organic material to make the space big enough for you to fit. Inspect the log for insects while you do this, as some species can do some serious damage with a bite. Also, note that if the log cleanings are dry enough they can be used as kindling to start a fire. Please see the next section for more on this.

Once the interior is cleaned, you can climb right in. Also, like with the tree and bushes, you may use debris, like leaves, to insulate the space.

Tarp Shelters

Also called a tarp tent, this is a nylon or plastic sheet used to create a makeshift tent. It is usually outfitted with poles, tent pegs, and guy lines. For added protection, I would use duct tape to seal the ends of the shelter. This is an item that will need to be in your emergency kit for you to make use of it, but it comes in mighty handy in keeping you dry and warm.

You have three options as to how to use the tarp shelter. One, you can drape this over a fallen tree or log. Keep the elements out by using a heavy rock to keep the ends to the ground. This makes a good temporary shelter for a day or two.

Two, you can gain more height by draping the tarp tent over a branch of a tree or a tall bush. This allows you to set up camp for longer and can be used for up to 7 days. This setup is great for hunting.

Three, you can use a rope to elevate the tent even higher on a tree. The added room allows you the convenience of building a small fire. This offers a longer stay than the first two options as long as you insulate the space to keep warm.

Snow Trenches

If you are exposed to the elements in cold conditions, such as a snowstorm, it is imperative that you not only find shelter but also keep as warm as possible. If you have none of the above-mentioned options available to you, you can use what nature is providing you plenty of just then—snow. This seems like an oxymoron, right? The idea of snow to keep warm and sheltered, but it is plausible once you know how to go about it the right way.

The solution is to build a snow trench. This is a hole dug out of the snow. It is about 3 feet deep and only slightly longer than the body it is meant to accommodate. (layer with pine boughs or space blanket. Never lay directly on the snow as it will soak your clothing and conduct body heat away quickly)

A snow trench, while it can never keep you toasty, it can keep you warm enough to survive the harsh conditions. This happens as your own body heat is trapped between the walls of snow and your body. The hole also keeps the wind out.

To create a snow trench, add branches, sticks, or any other stable roofing item to create a cover after the hole that has been dug up. Add a tarp, towels, blankets, plywood, or any similar and appropriate device to complete this covering. This should then be covered by snow to insulate the space. You can pad the inside with leaves, newspaper, plastic bags, or blankets for more warmth. Then all you have to do is slide in.

Lean-to

This temporary shelter uses a horizontal support beam constructed across the top and supported by branches or sticks. To create a lean-to, place a straight and hardened branch between two trees. Really any similar items, like wooden planks and ski poles, can serve the same purpose. Ideally, you will place this on the spots where branches form a "V" on these trees. You can also lash the main branch to the trees using cords. If you are constructing a smaller shelter, you can lean the branch on one tree and brace the other end on the ground.

Next, lean smaller branches along the sides of the shelter. This action is what gives the construct its name.

Insulate the shelter and make it rain-resistant by piling up debris along the frame from the ground going up. The thicker the layer of debris, the warmer the shelter will be. The tougher your lean-to construction, the longer it can be used. Some constructs give shelter for months.

Chapter 2 - Staying Warm

In moderate temperatures, typically, moving around is enough to generate enough body heat to keep you warm. That becomes more difficult when temperatures drop at night. You are no longer moving around, and your breathing slows down. Both of these conditions mean a drop in body temperature. As a result, you need to find a location where you can have dry shelter and good insulation. Of course, you should dress as warmly as possible in layers. Ways that you can generate even more warmth at night include:

Creating a Fire

Starting a fire is a handy skill to have, even outside of emergency situations. However, in a survival situation, knowing how to do that not only means that you have a source of warmth but also one of light and a way to cook food.

You need 3 main ingredients to start a fire: fuel, heat, and air. If any one of these ingredients is missing, then you will not have a fire. Let's look at the options available to you for each of these ingredients.

Your fuel sources are tinder, fuel wood, and kindling. Tinder is a highly flammable, dry material (such as an old birds nest, dry grasses, or even shredded paper), and certainly serves its purpose. Fuel wood, (also called firewood) as it is more commonly referred to is wood that has been harvested and combusts to generate heat. Kindling tends to be used to start a fire from tinder so that it burns long enough to ignite the bigger fuel wood. Kindling found naturally include twigs and small branches. Artificial options include cardboard. Fold this in the form of a small branch, and you should be all set.

The obvious choices for heat or igniting the fire are matches and lighters. Carry these in a waterproof container in your emergency kit. Using flint and steel, or a striker and ferrocerium rod, are also options for ignition. Friction can also be used to start a fire. Put learning hand drills and bow drills on your to-do list if you have not already acquired these skills.

Lastly, air is needed to create a fire. More specifically, you need the oxygen in the air that we breathe to start a fire. As the fuel source burns, oxygen reacts with the rest of the air compounds to release heat and generate other combustion items, like smoke and embers.

Now that you have all the ingredients needed to create a fire, the general steps for doing so include:
- Creating a dry space that is at least 3 feet wide. If you are starting a fire in the snow, dig to get to bare ground or create a platform with branches or logs.
- Create a wall to contain your fire. Use logs or rocks. Do not stack the wall too high or this will prevent the proper airflow needed to start the fire.
- Place a pile of tinder in the center of the space. Newspaper strips can be used in this instance. If used, create a loose ball to increase the surface area and the burning time.
- Brace the kindling against the tinder. Do not pack this on too tight.

- Light the tinder and gently blow to generate a flame from the spark.
- When the kindling catches on fire, add a few more pieces of kindling.
- When a good ember has been created, add the larger firewood.

Please note that a good fire can make it through a light downpour of rain. However, it is best to make a shelter before starting a fire in rainy conditions.

Tea Candles

Think of these as a candle in a cup, as this is what they resemble. They are normally small and circular. They contain a candle that liquifies in the holder so that it stays lit for longer. Because of their size and small weight, they are easy to keep in your emergency kit. Even though they are small, they emit a good amount of heat and light and are well suited for a small area. Be cautious while using tea candles though. They are open flames and can cause a fire if used carelessly or left unattended.

Survival Blankets

Survival blankets are a thin covering made out of metal and used particularly to keep people warm during emergencies. They do so by trapping heat, even in the coldest weather. They are light enough to keep stocked in your emergency kit but sturdy enough to fulfill the tasks. Here's a handy tip: they can be used to provide a temporary roof in a snow trench.

Newspapers or Plastic Sheets

Additions to this list include leaves, evergreen boughs, and plastic bags. They can be used to trap your body heat around you in times when a survival blanket is not available. They can also serve as sleeping mats.

Hand Warmers

These are an option to place in your emergency kit. They are flat devices that are small enough to place in your pocket. They contain material like hot liquid, chemical, or a heating element that is battery operated. They are designed specifically for heating hands. Luckily, they are relatively cheap and easy to use. They are particularly useful in times when it is hard to get a fire lit or if it is too dangerous to do so.

Hot Stones

These are the stones obtained from a fire after it no longer has an active flame. They are not actively burning but still generate enough heat to produce warmth. Place them around the area where you plan to slumber or close enough so that you feel their heat.

Passive Exercise

This keeps your blood flowing, so it keeps your body temperature up. It also helps keep the area around you warm. To practice passive exercise, all you have to do is contract and relax your muscles for a few minutes.

Passive exercise is best done while you are in a sleeping bag, but if you are surrounded by a snow trench, leaves, and branches, this also helps to generate enough body heat to keep you alive.

Chapter 3 - Cooling Off

Just as keeping warm can be a concern during an emergency, so can keeping cool. Of course, there are the obvious scenarios of being deserted in a desert or being removed from a cooler climate and having to adjust to one that is much hotter. But the need to find effective ways to cool down is a situation that many of us are dealing with no matter where we live.

Global warming has made it so that even locations that are used to cold weather are experiencing heat waves. The NOAA's 2021 Annual Climate Report combined land and ocean temperature and reported that there has been an average rate increase of 0.14 degrees Fahrenheit every decade since 1880. That translates into 0.08 degrees Celsius per decade. The statistic gets more troubling as this report also states the average rate of increase since 1981 is more than double those digits at 0.32°F (0.18°C).

That means higher temperatures everywhere on this planet. With increased temperatures comes higher humidity, energy and transport crises, a strain on the water supply, loss of crops and livestock, leading to food shortage and more. Higher temperatures also have heat-related effects on the body like respiratory and cardiovascular disorders. In the US, from 2004 to 2018, an average of 700 heat-related deaths occurred every year.

The responsibility is on you to protect yourself from these temperature increases. Actions that you can take include:

Avoiding the Sun

This might seem like an obvious tip, but it is astounding to note the number of hours many people spend outdoors in the sun doing tasks that can wait until there is less sun exposure. The sun is at its peak between 11 AM and 2 PM. While it is not always avoidable to be out between these times, you can actively schedule your time so that as few activities are done outdoors at that time. If you have to go outside when the sun is centered in the sky, use an umbrella and sunscreen and stick to shady spots as much as possible. I even dip into stores to make use of the A/C when I can to keep cool. While I am inside, I do some browsing. I have come across many interesting finds this way, as some of these places are not ones I normally frequent—an added benefit. Avoid exerting yourself while you are out. Take it slow and try not to work up a sweat.

Stay Hydrated

Staying hydrated, whether you are directly or indirectly in the sun, is the best way to beat the effects of the heat. It gives your cells the water they need to continue working optimally and replaces the water lost during sweating. To be clear, staying hydrated is something you must always do, whether in hot or cold weather. But when temperatures are higher, your body needs even more hydration. Adults need to drink 8 glasses of water every day to stay hydrated, and more during times of higher temperatures.

Ways that you can keep hydrated include:
- Keeping a water bottle close by and within your view.
- Placing reminders to drink water at regular intervals.
- Add ice drinks, like tea and juice.
- Eat fruits and vegetables with a high water concentration, like watermelon and cucumber.
- Add lemon or a leaf of mint to your water if you do not like the taste of water and struggle to drink it. Other fruit infusions, like berries and watermelon, are an option.
- Drink cool water between 40° and 50° F.

Avoid drinking energy drinks and sodas to hydrate, as they normally contain caffeine, which can harm your heart. Combined with the stress of heat on the body, this is a recipe for gaining a heat-related illness. Also, avoid drinking alcohol, as this causes dehydration.

Frozen Treats

This is quite the tasty way to keep cool. Frozen fruit smoothies, popsicles, ice creams, creamsicles, and more are all options. They also please your inner child. Just be sure to not overdo it on the sugary options.

Cooling Sheets and Pillows

The counterpart to warming sheets and pillows, these are an investment because they can be pricey, but they are well worth it. They are a great option for keeping cool in the nighttime, especially when you do not own an A/C unit in your living space.

Fans

Get cooler air circulating in your environment with the use of fans. There are many options. The first is the use of ceiling fans. Be sure to face the fans in the direction that causes the downward flow of air. Standing fans are also an option. They need to also be faced in a way that ensures the cooler air gets to the space it is needed most. Desk fans provide the option in a more professional environment, and electric hand fans allow you to get the cool air on the go since they are battery-operated.

Be sure to turn your fans off when you are not home so that you are conserving electricity, especially if blackouts and brownouts occur in your area.

Spray Bottles

These handy gadgets allow you to immediately cool your face and wrist with a simple spritz of water. Just keep the spray bottle filled with cool water nearby.

You can step your game up with the spray bottle by spraying your bed with water and aiming a fan at the mattress. This instantly cools the bed, and you can sleep comfortably. Just be sure not to drench the bed with water.

Book 20 – The Life-Saving Skills You Need

You never know when you'll be in an emergency situation and having the skills to get you out of it or safely settled until you can get the help is paramount. This section highlights the most important skills that you need and how you can develop them.

Chapter 1 - Life-Saving First-Aid Skills

Learning the following life-saving skills gives you the ability to save yourself and other people during SHTF events or even just during times when things go wrong:

Learning Cardiopulmonary Resuscitation (CPR)

This is a useful skill in situations where someone has suffered a heart attack or is suffering the consequences of a heart-related disease. Someone else manually pumps the blood and oxygen from the heart to the brain and other organs to keep the person alive until medical intervention is secured. CPR training allows you to learn the chest compression breath techniques needed.

The Automated External Defibrillator (AED)

CPR is used to keep blood flowing, but it does not restart the heart. In cases where the heart needs that jump-start, an AED is needed. It is recommended that a person be certified to use such a device, as they are normally located in places such as airports and shopping centers. However, during life-threatening situations, even without formal training, you can make use of these to save someone's life.

Checking for Signs of Life

The 2 most reliable signals that a person is alive are a pulse and breathing. The first thing that you should do when attending to someone who needs help is to ask if they are okay. If they do not respond, look for the rising and falling of the chest to indicate breathing. Next, place your index and middle finger against their inner wrist to check for a pulse. You can also check for a pulse by placing the same two fingers on the side of the neck, just below their jaw.

Using the Bandage

When used correctly, the use of bandages prevents blood loss. Use gloves before assisting anyone else when blood is involved and ensure that 911 has been called. This person should be lying down and covered with a blanket. Elevate the area that has been injured and wrap the appropriate length of bandage around the wound. Apply continuous pressure for 20 minutes then check to see if the bleeding has stopped.

If the bleeding has not ceased, continue to apply pressure to the wound with a large absorbent bandage or improvise with a folded shirt, towel, etc.

The Heimlich Maneuver

This is a technique used to save someone from choking. Luckily, you do not have to be certified to apply this maneuver. Start by standing behind the victim and delivering 5 hits to the middle of the back with the heel of your hand. Ideally, the item that is choking the person will be dislodged. If not, while standing behind them, wrap your hands around the person and make a fist between the navel and the bottom of the rib cage, place your other hand over the closed fist. Do 5 rapid abdominal thrusts while pulling their body back and up like you are trying to lift them off the ground.

First-Aid for Burning

Different burns have different degrees of severity. Namely, they are first-, second- and third-degree burns. First-degree burns are considered minor and can be treated by running the area under cold water for 10 minutes then gently apply a moist, cool compress. Never apply dressings or creams to burns. Pain can be treated with ibuprofen or acetaminophen. Second-degree burns are considered moderate, and third-degree burns are considered severe. These require medical care, and emergency personnel should be notified.

Save Someone from Drowning

The phrase "reach, throw, row, and go" can be used to memorize the technique to help someone who is drowning.

1. **Reach** by lying flat on the ground and using an item, such as a branch, to reach as far as you can extend. If the person grabs a hold, pull them toward you.
2. **Throw** a safety ring to the victim if it is available.
3. **Row** a boat to reach the victim if it is available.
4. **Go** is the last resort and should only be used in extreme circumstances if you are a skilled swimmer. Swim out to the victim and pull them to shore.

All of these life-saving skills can be learned from basic life-saving courses, so sign up for one today.

Chapter 2 - Life-Saving Skills in the Wilderness

Being in the throes of a life-threatening situation is not the time to think about learning life-saving skills. This must be done beforehand to give you the abilities you need to survive. If, and when, these trying times come to pass, you can feel confident in your ability to extend or lend a helping hand so that everyone involved is better off and safer. Survival skills I advise that you learn (apart from the skills listed above) include:

Keeping Fire Starters Handy

They can be used to start a fire, if need be, in wet and windy conditions. They are inexpensive, easy to use, and light enough to keep in your emergency kit.

Packing a Garbage Sack

A 42-gallon or 55-gallon garbage bag is an overlooked but handy item to keep in your emergency kit. They are almost as light as a feather, inexpensive, and take up a small amount of space. They can be used several ways: as a moisture barrier for bedding; as insulation after being filled with debris, like leaves; as a makeshift raincoat; to keep your gear dry; to collect water; and more.

Leaving Your Location in Trusted Hands

You, of course, want to protect your privacy, but someone else knowing your location can be the difference between life and death. If you leave for a trip outside of your normal routine, make sure that your last location is traceable. Send it to someone whom you trust or leave the details somewhere accessible in your home, like on your refrigerator.

Keeping Your Cell Phone Powered Up

Your cell phone is a handy survival tool. Apart from being a device that can be used to contact someone else for help, it can be used as a GPS, an educational tool to learn survival skills on the fly, to send an SOS, and more. Be sure to take a portable charger with you to keep this handy tool charged at all times.

Testing Your Gear Regularly

Do not leave it up to chance that your survival gear is still functioning when you need it most. Regularly conduct tests of these items to make sure they work. Set up a schedule for this so that it does not slip your mind.

Avoiding Hypothermia

Hypothermia represents a loss of body heat faster than the body can reproduce the temperature needed to ensure adequate functioning. Situations that can lead to developing hypothermia include staying in cold conditions too long, not wearing clothes appropriate for cold conditions, being prevented from moving to a warm dry location, not getting out of wet clothes or falling into water, such as in an accident or during a flood.

You can prevent this from happening to you by learning skills, such as how to build a fire, regularly checking the weather, layering up during outings, and how to find appropriate shelter to stay warm. You can also include items that prevent this and generate heat in your emergency kit. A lighter is one such example that is inexpensive and easy to use. Using waterproof clothing and shoes also comes in a clutch.

Always Bring Extra Clothes

Always plan for unexpected overnight stays by ensuring you will be sufficiently clothed. This is important especially when you take trips outdoors. When packing extra clothes, make sure they meet the criteria: they can keep you dry and warm.

Wool is a great insulating material. It is about 60% effective at retaining body heat. It will even retain your body heat when wet.

There are polyester materials that are windproof, as well as good insulators but will not retain body heat if wet.

Down is another great insulator, but those properties are lost when it becomes even slightly damp.

Cotton is not great for insulation but rather good for keeping you cool. Cotton will NOT retain body heat when wet. In fact, this is the worst choice for staying warm in wet conditions. Wet blue jeans are responsible for many cases of hypothermia and death.

You need to understand the environment that you would be in and what clothes are best suited for it. You also need to keep extra clothing in case what you are wearing becomes dirty or damaged.

Chapter 3 - Marking Your Waypoints

Waypoints are a point of reference that allow you to note your location. While they can be by specific longitude and latitude marks, buildings and natural features can also serve as waypoints. Develop your navigation skills by noting these both in urban and rural environments in your everyday life.

Be aware of your surroundings. This allows navigation skills to develop naturally. This gauge of location becomes automatic so that when you need it most, you can accurately recall the distance to your destination or to potential places where you can find help.

Learning the Identities of Trees

Different trees have different purposes. Some tree parts, like that of pine and birch, are useful for building and tinder. Others are useful for holding dry leaves that can be useful for insulation. Beech trees are an example of this. Others can be foraged and their parts eaten. Developing knowledge of these specific trees, and other types of foliage, is about studying those that are popular in your area and making it a point to increase your knowledge about them.

Knapping a Knife

Knapping refers to the process of breaking or chipping away at something with sharp blows so that it forms a specific shape to perform a specific function. Knapping a knife is the act of chipping away at a material, like a rock, to develop a knife-like shape. Knives are a mighty useful survival tool.

Keeping a Personal Locator Beacon on Your Person

Sometimes, time is a critical factor that determines whether or not a person lives or dies. In such circumstances, getting emergency assistance as quickly as possible is paramount. Personal Locator Beacons (PLBs) are devices that send distress calls to emergency personnel so that they can assist as quickly as possible. Keep one on your person so you can get help as quickly as possible if such a situation arises.

Lighting a Road Flare when Needed

Road flares are an item that should be kept in your emergency kit, as they have a variety of uses and can be used in extreme situations, such as in rain or snow. They can be used for illumination, as a defensive measure, as a heat source, and as a distress signal. (do not use road flares in an enclosed area. They put out toxic smoke and displace oxygen)

Using a Reflective Blanket

Reflective blankets are small and highly portable. You can use one simply in an emergency situation by wrapping it around your body to keep warm. The reflective material captures body heat and reflects it back to you. You can also use these insulating properties by adding it to your sleeping bag or laying up on the ground. In such a case, the blanket captures heat from the earth and conducts it to your body. Reflective blankets can also be a distress signal as they are bright and shiny.

Insulating Yourself

If you are trapped out in the wilderness and man-made gear is not available to you, items around you can be used to keep warm. Dry leaves, tree boughs, and pine needles can be gathered and kept close to you as a natural barrier against the elements.

Repurposing Water Bottles

If you are out in the wilderness and have emptied out a plastic water bottle, do not be so quick to discard it. It can be used for other survival tasks with a few simple modifications. Cut a hole into the bottle cap, fill the bottle with clean, sterilized water, and put the cap back in place. When the bottle is squeezed, water is squirted from the cap at high pressure. This can be used for personal hygiene, such as washing your hands or cleaning a wound.

Learning How to Recycle Shotgun Shells

The shells of a 12-gauge shotgun make great survival tools all on their own. They can be used as holders for candles or other items, such as matches, tinder, and fishing tools, or as a first-aid kit companion in which antibacterial ointments and bandages can be kept. Place a candle wick in a spent shotgun shell. Fill this with melted wax. This creates a fire starter that ignites even wet. Cover these with reflective tape to make them easier to spot.

Learning How to Create a Fire from Chips

Chips are a great companion with your favorite sandwich, but they can also be used to create a fire because the flammable oil along their surface can serve as fuel. As a survival mechanism, they can be used to prepare food that is healthier for you.

The Search and Rescue Signal

Barring circumstances where there is an immediate danger that prevents you from staying in your current location, if you are caught out in the wild and cannot navigate your way back to safety, it is best to sit and wait for rescue. Reduce the time that it takes emergency personnel to get to you by creating a search and rescue signal in the form of a fire. It alerts others to your location through the sight of the fire, which can be noted day and night, and the smell of the smoke.

To create this search and rescue signal, create a fire and place damp or green material on it so that a cloud of white smoke is created. If greenery is not available, such as in snowy conditions, throw an oil-based product, like a plastic water bottle, on the fire. This creates a black smoke that certainly stands out against the white of a snow-covered location.

If you are indeed using a search and rescue signal, ensure that it is controlled so that you don't threaten your life or cause an expanding fire.

Chapter 4 - Life-Saving Skills for Weapons and Protection

Protect yourself and those that matter to you with the following skill development:

Learn to Create Your Own Weapon

From simple sticks to more sophisticated defenses, learning to make a weapon is not only defense against dangerous humans but also against animals that can cause bodily harm.

Make Candles

Candles are a source of heat and light. They are great resources when the power is out, and they are great for the environment, as they burn clean. Learning to make them is simple.

Make a Rope

Ropes can be used to secure an intruder or someone else who threatens your safety, as fencing material to keep your residency safe, while camping or fishing, and in a variety of circumstances. Luckily, you can make a rope out of several types of material.

Learn to Sew

We are used to simply going out to a store to buy new clothes or bringing the items to a seamstress or tailor for repair. But in survival situations, these resources may not be available to us. Learn to stitch, repair, and patch clothes in addition to making them from scratch.

Learn to Knit

This is not the pastime for ideal grandmas. Instead, learning the skill allows you the ability to create your own clothes and other useful items.

Learn to Make a Basket

Baskets can be used to store and gather food, clothes, tools, and more; as bowls and plates; to catch waste; during hunting and fishing; and other survival activities, like cooking, gathering and sifting seeds, and drying meats fruits and vegetables.

Chapter 5 - Life-Saving Skills for Food

Learning such skills allows you to diversify your food resources with the acquisition, growth, and production of your own food. Skill sets that you can develop include:

Hunting

Under this heading, you need to learn the powers of observation and patience, navigation, marksmanship, stalking, and shooting a gun, to name a few. Hunting also requires both mental and physical fitness and toughness.

Trapping and Snaring

The goal of trapping and snaring is to capture, contain, and kill game that you have identified as food. As a result, you need to know and understand the chosen animals. Supplement this by learning bushcraft, the tools of the trade and how to set traps

Fishing

Reading the water, baiting, reeling, casting, and setting traps are all sub-skills within this category that should be pursued.

Gardening

Some skills that can help you plan, plant, and harvest healthy crops from your garden include learning to plant in small spaces, bucket gardening, composting, soil analysis, sun tracking, plant propagation from techniques, like stem cutting, pest control, pollination, seed germination, and the building of planter boxes

Chapter 6 - Extra Life-Saving Skills

To close this section, I am providing a few more skills that I think will be worth your time and effort to learn. They include:

Learning to Tie a Knot

Learning this skill can be useful in a variety of ways, such as aiding in anchoring a shelter, carrying heavy loads, like firewood, hanging food bags, and hunting.

Fighting and Self-Defense

Learning to physically protect yourself can be useful in situations of civil unrest and personal safety compromises like during home invasions and robberies.

Learning to Use a Firearm

Having an accident while having a firearm places you and other people at unnecessary risk. Firearms ownership is a serious responsibility, and it is the responsibility of the owner to learn to use it properly and wisely.

Learning a New Language

You never know if you will be placed in a new environment where the people and their culture and language are different, so it is a good pastime to learn a new language and about the cultures associated with that language. Knowing the language in a different setting allows you to communicate more effectively and potentially avoid confrontations. It is also a means of getting more resources. Learning another language also has benefits, like aiding in your career and providing mental exercise.

There you have it! The full guide on how to survive in some of the worst disasters in the world is at your fingertips at any time that you need a refresher.

Leave a 1 click review!

SINCE SELF-PUBLISHERS REALLY DEPEND ON READERS' REVIEWS, I WOULD BE INCREDIBLY GRATEFUL IF YOU COULD TAKE 60 SECONDS TO WRITE A BRIEF REVIEW ON AMAZON, EVEN IF JUST A FEW SENTENCES.
PLEASE SCAN THE QR CODE BELOW TO LEAVE A REVIEW. THANK YOU!

Conclusion

I know lots of people who used to believe that zombie apocalypses and alien invasions are the stuff that science-fiction is made of. After all, many of our childhoods were filled with watching the portrayals on television with a bowl of popcorn and laughter, thinking how silly but how entertaining. We also used to think that global pandemics were a thing that we left in the past, when technology and medicine were not so advanced. We are making strides in both of these things and they should not be a worry, right?

However, 2020 showed us how wrong that assumption was. Just as the sudden but far-reaching effects of Covid-19 has shown us all, a pandemic is a real thing and it could happen at any time. Any and every one of us could be affected directly or indirectly. Many of us lost loved ones. Many of us contracted the virus and were ill. Some of those who were ill are still suffering consequences to this day. Some of us lost our jobs because of the pandemic and were left without an income and a way to support ourselves and our families. Some of us were faced with the possibility of homelessness. We had to readjust and continue to adjust to a new way of living with homeschooling, remote working, shopping for items we were used to picking up at the grocery store, and so many more changes.

Preppers Can Make It Through The Unfathomable

Some people were not affected as heavily by the fallout of the Covid-19 pandemic because they were prepared for the worst-case scenario. Their pantries were stocked. They were not worried when grocery shelves were wiped clean in the blink of an eye. They were not panicking when food and medicines were on short, and even no, supply. Many had multiple streams of income that did not depend on them going to a physical location to earn them. While they might not have been comfortable with the situation—and of course, affected just like everyone else—they were physically prepared to withstand it better than the majority of people. They were certainly more mentally braced than the masses.

Being prepared gives you peace of mind. Being in that constant readiness gives you the confidence to live everyday life to its fullest because not only are you aware of just how precious every second is but you also understand that things could change at any moment, spelling the end of the world as we know it ... and you can adjust to those changes because you have put strategies in place beforehand.

Preppers are generally ready to face the challenges of life. Wars. Natural disasters. Food and water shortage. Pandemics. All of these SHTF events are not limited to movies and books. At any second, on any given day of the week, they can turn from fiction into reality. Preppers are more likely to survive them.

Preppers have better mental health, which usually translates into better physical health. Because they actively prepare for the worst, they rest easier when they lay their heads down on a pillow at night. They are not worried and stressed about the possibilities. They are not trying to figure out how to feed their families, or gain access to medicine, or protect their homes from intruders if the world comes crashing down around them. Why? Because they have already taken measures to mitigate those circumstances if that is what they wake up to.

While the negative connotations associated with preppers are nervous, paranoid individuals, the truth of the matter is that they are:

- Self-confident
- Financially suave
- Self-sufficient and able to do more with less
- At peace

Why? Because they know they can handle life or death situations, and their level of preparedness has given them a more likely opportunity to make it out alive in that situation.

Anyone Can Be A Prepper

You can become a prepper at any time, and if you already are, you can gain more knowledge and skills to up your preparedness game. You no longer have to be dependent on the government or emergency officials to save you. You can become completely self-reliant. You can become part of the solution and make a positive impact on society, especially in times of trouble. You become wiser about the bad things that can happen in life. Therefore, take steps to thrive and survive during such times. That is the future you have ahead of you as a prepper.

And it all starts with a decision. You have to make the choice to embrace the peppers' lifestyle and the shift in perspective that comes with it. The great thing? You can make that choice any time. You can make it right now. Next, all you have to do is follow those thoughts up with action and the commitment to learn more.

What Are Preppers Preparing to Survive?

Living life is challenging. It can send blow after blow your way. You can fall to the ground and continue to take these hits, hoping they will stop or you can stand your ground and learn to defend yourself and fight, landing a few hits of your own.

Preppers learn to fight back by evaluating the risks and noting their strengths and weaknesses to classify their vulnerabilities. From there, they develop strategies to mitigate the possible damages they will suffer from these risks.

The common risks (SHTF situations) that have been highlighted in this book include:
- Health hazards like pandemics
- Natural disasters, like earthquakes, tsunamis, tornados, heat waves, droughts, hurricanes, floods, and wildfires
- Man-made disasters, like war, terrorism, and cyberattacks
- Financial troubles, like unemployment, economic collapse, and recession
- Social unrest, like home invasions, looting, and burglary

To lower your risk, this book outlines:
- The proper way to store, preserve, and prepare food
- How to obtain and store water
- How to defend your person, your loved ones, your home, and your material possessions
- How to use natural and pharmaceutical medicines to heal yourself and keep healthy
- How to live off the grid
- What to do during SHTF events to ensure your survival
- Life-saving skills everyone should know

Gene Penaflor survived even though he had been stranded in the wilderness with no food or water for almost 3 weeks. José Salvador Alvarenga spent 13 months drifting the high seas, and he survived to tell the tale because he was resourceful and determined to live. Laronda Marshall and Matt Uber saved the lives of others by using life-saving techniques instead of panicking. Keith Callahan and his wife adapted to living in a shed and removed themselves from underneath the burden of the financial headache of a mortgage. Kirsten Jacobsen moved to New Mexico to help build her own Earthship home, created from recycled material, like aluminum cans and tires, and is doing her part to help save the planet while living self-sufficiently. The residents of Dancing Rabbit have integrated wind turbines and solar arrays to be even more eco-friendly and less dependent on the "grid."

These are people who, in one way or the other, highlight the success that can be obtained from being prepared to deal with an emergency or diverging from the status quo and living more self-sufficiently.

Preppers were typically mocked before 2020, but then the pandemic hit and the merit of preparation was learned. They became a resource for their wealth of knowledge and skills.

We do not have to wait to learn the hard way. Starting today, you can start preparing yourself for the future and what may come. Even the odds of this happening are low. Once it is not zero, there is cause to be ready to deal with it. Lead by example and give a sustainable life to you and your family.

The more people who adopt the mindset of preparedness before the worst happens, the less of a burden all of us as a global society will have to recover. Help your neighbor, someone else across the international map, and perhaps a nameless face across the internet will find the same sentiments that you have in this book by leaving a review. It goes a long way in helping the people who need this book the most find it.

Thank you for leaving that recommendation and for picking up this book in the first place. Congratulations on reaching the end, as it shows your commitment to this lifestyle. Good luck on this life journey of preparation and readiness!

FREE GIFT TO OUR READER

PREPPER'S JOURNAL
PDF DOWNLOAD

References

Survival World. "10 Best Canned Foods for Survival." (2021, December 24). Retrieved from https://www.survivalworld.com/food/canned-foods-for-survival/

Edwards, Rebecca. "8 Surprising Home Burglary Facts and Stats." Safewise. (2022, May 20). Retrieved from https://www.safewise.com/blog/8-surprising-home-burglary-statistics/

Bradford Metropolitan District Council. (n.d.). "How to Prepare for Climate Change." (2022). Retrieved from https://www.bradford.gov.uk/environment/climate-change/how-to-prepare-for-climate-change/

CDC. "Heat-related deaths — United States, 2004–2018." (2020, June 17). Retrieved from https://www.cdc.gov/mmwr/volumes/69/wr/mm6924a1.htm#:~:text=During%202004%E2%80%932018%2C%20an%20average,alcohol%20poisoning%2C%20and%20drug%20overdoses

History.com Editors. "5 Stunning Real-Life Survival Stories. (2019, June 5). Retrieved from https://www.history.com/news/5-stunning-real-life-survival-stories

NCEI. Monitoring.Info@noaa.gov. (n.d.). "Global Climate Report - Annual 2021." Retrieved from https://www.ncei.noaa.gov/access/monitoring/monthly-report/global/202113

Centers, Josh. "New Statistics on Modern Prepper Demographics from FEMA and Cornell." Start Prepping. (2021, August 10). Retrieved from https://theprepared.com/blog/new-statistics-on-modern-prepper-demographics-from-fema-and-cornell-university/#:~:text=That%20grew%20to%204.5%25%20in,million%20number%20we%20often%20estimate

CDC. "Preparing for a Hurricane or Other Tropical Storm." (2020, July 29). Retrieved from https://www.cdc.gov/disasters/hurricanes/before.html

SafeHome.org Team. "Property Crime in America: 2006-2021." SafeHome.org. (2021, August 20). Retrieved from https://www.safehome.org/safest-cities/#:~:text=In%202019%20alone%2C%20American%20homes,state%2C%20and%20federal%20law%20enforcement

Saragosa, M. "Why 'Preppers' are Going Mainstream." BBC News (2020, December 10). Retrieved from https://www.bbc.com/news/business-55249590

www.ingramcontent.com/pod-product-compliance
Lightning Source LLC
Chambersburg PA
CBHW081707100526
44590CB00022B/3689